W9-BWP-005

The Theatre Of Pilgrimage

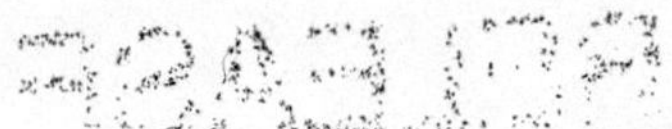

ST. JOSEPH'S UNIVERSITY STX
PN1821.F4 The theatre of pilgrimage.
3 9353 00148 0316

The Theatre Of Pilgrimage

by Ernest Ferlita

PN
1821
F4

142320

SHEED AND WARD NEW YORK

For my mother,
and then for youree,
franklin and c.j.

Chapter One, "The Theatre of Pilgrimage,"
originally appeared in *New Orleans Review.*

© Sheed and Ward, Inc., 1971

Library of Congress Catalog Card Number: 72-125831

Standard Book Number: 8362-1065-4 (Library Edition)
8362-0489-1 (Paperback)

Manufactured in the United States of America

Contents

	ACKNOWLEDGMENTS	vii
I.	THE THEATRE OF PILGRIMAGE	1
II.	KING LEAR	13
III.	THE ROAD TO DAMASCUS	34
IV.	THE COCKTAIL PARTY	59
V.	BREAK OF NOON	80
VI.	CAMINO REAL	95
VII.	HUNGER AND THIRST	111
VIII.	THE FUGITIVE	126
IX.	MY KINSMAN, MAJOR MOLINEUX	137
	CONCLUSION	150
	APPENDIX: Related Readings	154
	BIBLIOGRAPHY	165

Acknowledgments

This book comes at the end of my four years at the Yale School of Drama. I wish to thank Richard Gilman, Professor of Drama, for giving me, through discussion, a sense of the road; Howard Stein, Associate Dean, for challenging my work at regular intervals; Jan Kott, Visiting Professor of Drama, for reading with equanimity even those chapters in which I take issue with his view as put forth in *Shakespeare Our Contemporary;* Charles Prouty, Professor of English Language and Literature, for his critical interest in my analysis of *King Lear;* John McCall, S.J., for dropping a hint that led me into my topic; Fred Tollini, S.J., for companionship and argument, especially during the difficult first chapter; Juliana D'Amato, O.P., for another point of view; Donald Gelpi, S.J., and Joseph Tetlow, S.J., for reading, with the bravery of brothers, the completed work.

ERNEST FERLITA, S.J.

New Orleans, 1969

I. THE THEATRE OF PILGRIMAGE

Just before his attempted suicide Gauguin completed a large painting. In the foreground is a Polynesian woman reaching up to pick a fruit from a branch. She is flanked by the golden bodies of other native women, reclining with their children, and a few animals. In the background, at the left, a blue idol waits with arms uplifted; at the right, draped in rosy robes, two women (or is one a man?) walk in deep conversation. As they glide by, in the words of the artist, "a figure seated on the ground, disproportionately large, and intentionally so, raises an arm and stares in astonishment at these two people who dare think of their destiny."[1] The title of this remarkable painting preserves its sense of mystery: *Where Do We Come From? What Are We? Where Are We Going?*

These three questions have been asked over and over again in the theatre. Whenever they are asked, implicitly or explicitly, one can speak of a theatre of pilgrimage, a theatre in which man, hidden from himself, looks for his meaning not only in remembrance of the past and attention to the present but also in expectation of the future.

Strictly speaking, the Theatre of Pilgrimage is to be found only in the Judaeo-Christian tradition. "What being, with only one voice, has sometimes two feet, sometimes three, sometimes four, and is weakest when it has the most?" Oedipus solved the riddle of the sphinx by answering simply, Man. In Sophocles' play, the answer moves into deeper questioning: Who am *I*? To find out, Oedipus delves into the past: Where do I come from? When he cries, Where am I going? (l. 1310), he is already blind. Tom F. Driver explains:

In the *Oedipus Tyrannus* the future is closed. One might almost say that it does not exist. The time significance of the play must be understood entirely in terms of the relation between present and past. The past is dominant. It contains the facts which explain the present, which control the present; and the play, as it moves forward in time through the events of the terrible day, actually moves backward into the completely decisive past.[2]

It is quite otherwise in Calderón's *Life Is a Dream*. Segismundo, like Oedipus, had been put away in an attempt to cheat fate: An oracle had foretold that he would topple his father from his throne. Many years later, when he finds himself restored to his rightful place, he asks in amazement, Who am I? The answer comes to him out of the past. He is what the oracle foretold, "a mixture of man and beast" (II, 1), destined to trample his father. But when he asks, Where am I going? the past is not at all decisive. Having humbled his father, he does not play the beast but says instead: "Sire, arise! Give me your hand." "My son," Basilio exclaims, "so noble an action gives you new birth in my heart" (III, 3). The answer to the question Who am I? is only partially provided by the past; the rest lies in the future.

To say that *Life Is a Dream* is theatre of pilgrimage and *Oedipus Tyrannus* is not is to say nothing about the superiority of one play over the other. Both are powerful expressions of their respective traditions. In comparing them, all I intend is to locate the Theatre of Pilgrimage in the Judaeo-Christian tradition as distinct from the Greek.

We find it there mainly because of the way in which the former records the experience of time. This experience of time distinguishes the Judaeo-Christian not only from the Greek but also from the Oriental tradition. The experience is one of linear time as opposed to cyclic.

Much has been written in the attempt to explicate this opposition. In Greek thought, says Oscar Cullman, "time is not conceived as a progressing line with beginning and end, but rather as a circle," so that man experiences time "as an enslavement, as a curse."[3] Mircea Eliade writes at length about "the myth of eternal return" in the Greco-Oriental world, in which "everything begins over again at its commencement every instant. The past is but a prefiguration of the future."[4] But in the Judaeo-Christian world, the past is the point of departure into a future always open. Fearful of the future, Moses cries out: "Who am I?" (Exod. 3:11). But the only answer God gives is, "I will be with you." "This does not tell man what he was and what he really is," comments Jürgen Moltmann, "but what he will be and can be in that history and that future to which the mission leads him."[5] Some writers, though they continue to refer to this movement through time as linear, object to the term as too spatial. "Hebrew and Christian time is more interior and psychological," says Walter Ong.[6] Indeed, this qualification is quite in accord with what Christopher Dawson regards as the first formulation of the meaning of Judaeo-Christian time, that of St. Augustine: "Time is spiritual extension" (*Confessions,* XI, 27). "Thus the past is the soul's remembrance, the future is its expectation, and the present is its attention."[7]

Having set up this essential opposition between linear and cyclic time, it must be said at once that in the existential order the experience of one does not preclude the experience of the other. There is often a tension between them, and this will very definitely have its importance for the Theatre of Pilgrimage. To leave the "straight way" for the "wheel" is something both feared and desired. Even Nietzsche, with his profound historical sense, "could not escape the terrifying vision of The Return of All Things," Dawson remarks, "even if it seemed to nullify his own evolutionary gospel of the superman."[8]

> And this slow spider that crawls in the moonlight and this moonlight itself, and you and I whispering together in the gateway, must we not all have been before?
>
> And must we not come again and run that other long road before us—that long shadowy road—must we not return eternally?

What Nietzsche feared, Joyce and Eliot desired. Their work, Eliade believes, "is saturated with nostalgia for the myth of eternal repetition."[9] Ong describes how a cyclic view of human phenomena is still likely to assert itself "with owlish kindliness in a person such as Yeats, ironically and comically in James Joyce, militantly and ambivalently in Wyndham Lewis's Vorticist movement, furtively and somewhat noncommittally in T. S. Eliot."[10] And so, even in the Judaeo-Christian tradition, where the thrust is mainly linear, the whirlpool exercises its pull, either through one's natural propensities or through categories of Greek thought still at work in our culture.

In the Greek tradition the obverse is true: Though the movement is mainly cyclic, there is also a pull forward. Perhaps this pull is felt more strongly in Aeschylus than in Sophocles or Euripides. Cyclic time was an essential element in the world-view that they shared; but Aeschylus, in the *Oresteia,* dramatized the *evolution* of that world-view in the minds of men. There is, therefore, a linear thrust in the trilogy, and though it carries with it no momentum into a historical future, it nevertheless lifts man from the wheel of blind retribution and sets him down in a court of justice. There are, of course, references to a general future ("There shall be peace forever," in the last lines of the Chorus), but the reason why the linear thrust in the trilogy carries no momentum into a historical future is that Orestes, the one person whose particular history might have carried such momentum, is dismissed from the stage before the final resolution of the play—a clear indication, as Driver says, that the interest lies elsewhere.[11] Kitto concludes that in Greek drama one thing is constant:

> the assertion of a world-order, symbolized by the presence or activity of the gods. Sometimes, as in the *Oresteia* and *Prometheia,* the poet shows this order in evolution. Sophocles shows it in operation. In Euripides it is often presented by implication rather than directly: it consists in a due balance of forces . . .[12]

Where the prevailing view of time is linear, the pull toward cyclic time comes in the form of temptation. Where the prevailing view of time is cyclic, the pull toward linear time comes in the form of aspiration.

The experience of linear time in the Theatre of Pilgrimage is not to be confused with the linear plotting of a play, "well made" or otherwise. Linear time is evolutionary, or even revolutionary. It suggests that the phenomenon of man is unfinished, that the end will be different from the beginning. It is true, as Marshall McLuhan never lets us forget, that our "lineal perspectives" are changing, that "we live electrically in an instantaneous world," but this in no way means that we have reverted to cyclic time. "In this age of space-time we seek multiplicity, rather than repeatability of rhythms. This is the difference between marching soldiers and ballet."[13] It is not the difference between going forward and going in circles: On his way to the temple, David *danced* before the Ark, he did not march.[14]

In the Theatre of Pilgrimage, sin is best understood in terms of linear time. When I refer to sin in this context, I am speaking objectively, prescinding from any question of guilt. I use the word in its broadest sense, as synonymous with disorder. Again, the Greek theatre offers a contrast that may be useful. If, as Kitto shows, the trilogies of Aeschylus dramatize the growth of human society within an unalterable framework, then sin, for Aeschylus, is to give another revolution to the wheel of blind retribution, to exact blood for blood, and thus to retard the evolution toward world-order. If Sophocles dramatizes the operation of that world-order, then sin, for Sophocles, is to stand in the path of the inexorable wheel of *Dikê,* whether this be Justice or the ordained rhythm of things. If, for Euripides, world-order implies a due balance of forces, "such as for example of Aphrodite and Artemis, or Reason and Ecstasy, or the Rational and the Irrational,"[15] then sin is to stand absolutely on one side of the polarity and to turn one's back on the other side. For all three, sin is best understood in terms of cyclic time, which the assertion of a world-order governed by unalterable laws implies.

Sin, viewed in the Theatre of Pilgrimage in terms of linear time, is either a breaking out of time ("I wished this world's eternity," says the repentant Eleanor, banished for her intrigues, in the Second Part of *Henry the Sixth),* or a yielding to the weight of time (which was Hamlet's temptation: "O that this too too solid flesh would melt"). To sin by breaking out of time is to arrogate to oneself a kind of eternity, to "make sure of things." Hans Urs von Balthasar elaborates:

> Both Irenaeus and Clement [theologians of the early Church] consider that original sin consisted in anticipation of this kind; and indeed, at the close of Revelation the reward which the Son bestows upon the victor is that fruit of Paradise which the

sinner had to his own hurt stolen in anticipation (Apocalypse 2:7). God intended man to have *all* good, but in his, God's time. . . .

Seen in this perspective, sin consists essentially in breaking out of time.

Hence the restoration of order by the Son of God had to be the annulment of that premature snatching at knowledge, the beating down of the hand outstretched towards eternity, the repentant return from a false, swift transfer into eternity to a true, slow confinement in time.[16]

On the other hand, to sin by yielding to the weight of time "consists not so much in the titanic desire to be as God, but in weakness, timidity, weariness, not wanting to be what God requires of us."[17] This is the other aspect of man's "original sin," a settling for something less than God has in store for him, or even a settling for nothing: a sin of omission as opposed to one of commission, despair as opposed to presumption. Both forms constitute a sin against hope:

Presumption is a premature, self-willed anticipation of the fulfilment of what we hope for from God. Despair is the premature, arbitrary anticipation of the non-fulfilment of what we hope for from God. Both forms of hopelessness . . . cancel the *wayfaring* character of hope [Italics mine]. They rebel against the patience in which hope trusts in the God of promise. They demand impatiently either fulfilment "now already" or "absolutely no" hope.[18]

Hope, then, is an important element in the Theatre of Pilgrimage. By hope I do not mean the kind of optimism that resolves all contradictions by a blind leap into the future. Nor do I mean the kind of expectation that narrows the future by setting up its own conditions. By hope I mean that act by which man accepts the unfulfilled in himself as something implied in the very openness that defines him, involving him in the inner workings of a certain creative process. "Hope," says Gabriel Marcel, phenomenologically speaking, "is engaged in the weaving of experience now in process, or in other words in an adventure now going forward." Despair, he adds, "is in a certain sense the consciousness of time as closed or, more exactly still, of time as a prison—whilst hope appears as piercing through time; everything happens as though time, instead of hedging consciousness round, allowed something to pass through it."[19] Theologically speaking, Karl Rahner says that "one knows who God is and who man is only when he hopes, that is, when he bases his life on the unfathomable as his salvation . . . Whoever abandons himself to what is absolutely unfathomable abandons himself to his salvation. Whereas presumption *and* despair in the same way refuse to abandon themselves to what is unfathomable."[20]

Generally speaking, the importance of hope for characters in a pilgrimage play is in direct proportion to the imminence of death. When Everyman comes face to face with Death, and is commanded to go on a pilgrimage "which he in no wise can escape," he looks back upon his life, and seeing how he has squandered it, despairs. "Alas that ever I was born." On the other hand, although Faust, in Goethe's great work, has spent his life in the pursuit of learning, he is faced with "the impossibility of knowledge," and in despair decides to commit suicide. Just as he raises the poisoned cup, a chorus of voices announcing "the first glad hour of Easter" draws it away from his lips. But "wild dreams" continue to frighten him in his sleep and despair turns into presumption. "A curse on hope, a curse on faith, a curse, above all, on patience!" And he joins hands with Mephistopheles.

Everyman yields to the weight of time made heavy with self-indulgence, but at the last moment repents and rescues a few good deeds. Faust breaks out of time "to reach that crown of humanity for which all his senses yearn." He makes a pact with his own devil; or, in Nietzsche's terms, marries good and evil in himself "in order to arrive at the point that is beyond good and evil because it is the source of them both—the Self in its craving to live and grow."[21] Will his presumption damn him? "Man, in his striving, is ever prone to err." So says the God of the Prologue, when he gives Mephistopheles a free hand to tempt man's spirit. "He may journey in the dark, but instinctively he travels toward the light."

Faust and Everyman: they stand as archetypes for characters in the Theatre of Pilgrimage—characters who, like the couple in Gauguin's painting, "dare think of their destiny." Where do we come from? What are we? Where are we going? Others may say, "Asking gets you nowhere. Move." But they cannot help themselves, they must pause to ask questions and the others must either bear with them or trample them. When the answer comes in such a way that hope proves greater than despair, or mystery greater than problem, or the future greater than the past, even if only by a little, we have been given theatre of pilgrimage.

So far I have spoken of the Theatre of Pilgrimage in a broad sense. For purposes of this study, it will be necessary to narrow things somewhat. The very term Theatre of Pilgrimage already implies a journey through time in search of answers to questions that man's being poses. But there are some plays that make *explicit* use of the metaphor of journey or pilgrimage. I do not mean that the structure of the play is literally that of a pilgrimage, though it may be, but rather that the metaphor of pilgrimage is used to tell us something about man's search for meaning. In some plays it will be the main metaphor; in others it may be used only once, but in such a way that we are invited to view the entire action of the play in terms of it.[22] Obviously, the mere use of a "pilgrimage" word (such as *journey* or *road),* whether in the title of the play or in the text, is not enough to establish a play as theatre of pilgrimage in the strict sense. In Marc Connelly's *The Traveler,* the word *traveler* is never meant to function metaphorically. In each case, the play itself must be consulted.

I have been guided in my choice of plays by the variety of things they have to tell us about pilgrimage. I hope I have not forced them to tell. I feel, rather, that they have forced me to listen. *King Lear* tells what is possible in the valley of the human, at that level where light is no more. *The Road to Damascus* traces the ups and downs of the human spirit in its movement toward light. *The Cocktail Party* looks down two roads that diverge in a yellow wood. *Break of Noon* cuts across the desert of four lives, exposing them all to a blazing sun. *Camino Real* descends into a hell where the springs of humanity have gone dry. *Hunger and Thirst* uproots the heart and flings it to the winds. *The Fugitive* troubles the air with the sound of implacable footsteps. *My Kinsman, Major Molineux* stands ambivalently on the road to freedom.

And so our pilgrimage begins: Where do we come from? What are we? Where are we going?

NOTES

[1] *Lettre de Gauguin à Monfreid, février, 1898,* as quoted in *Gauguin* by Georges Wildenstein (Paris: Éditions les Beaux-Arts, 1964), p. 232.

[2] *The Sense of History in Greek and Shakespearean Drama*

(New York & London: Columbia University Press, 1967), pp. 166–67. In this excellent study, Driver compares *Oedipus Tyrannus* and *Macbeth, The Persians* and *Richard III,* the *Oresteia* and *Hamlet* and *Alcestis* and *The Winter's Tale.*

[3] *Christ and Time* (Philadelphia: Westminster Press, 1950), p. 52.

[4] *Cosmos and History* (New York: Harper Torchbooks, 1959), p. 89.

[5] *Theology of Hope* (New York: Harper & Row, 1967), p. 285.

[6] *In the Human Grain* (New York: Macmillan Co., 1967), p. 71.

[7] *Dynamics of World History* (New York: Sheed & Ward, 1956), p. 319.

[8] *Dynamics of World History,* p. 271, with quote from *Thus Spoke Zarathustra,* 30:2.2.

[9] *Cosmos and History,* p. 153.

[10] *In the Human Grain,* p. 93.

[11] *The Sense of History in Greek and Shakespearean Drama,* pp. 122–23, 136–38.

[12] H. D. F. Kitto, *Form and Meaning in Drama* (New York: University Paperbacks, 1960), p. 238.

[13] *Understanding Media: The Extensions of Man* (New York: McGraw-Hill Book Co., 1965), p. 149.

[14] Eliade reminds us that, by the very fact that it is a religion, Christianity had to keep at least one aspect of the cyclic-liturgical time, that is, the periodical recovery of the "beginnings." "However, though liturgical Time is a circular Time, Christianity, as faithful heir to Judaism, accepts the linear Time of History: the World was created only once and will have only one end; the Incarnation took place only once, in historical Time, and there will be only one Judgment." As faithful heir of Judaism, Christianity also "historicized" a certain number of seasonal festivals and cosmic symbols by connecting them with important events in her history (*Myth and Reality,* pp. 168–70). The tension between liturgical time and linear time is the tension between the priest and the prophet—a tension that operates within the context of an alliance. Cf. Driver, pp. 53–55.

[15] Kitto, p. 77.

[16] *A Theology of History* (New York: Sheed & Ward, 1963), p. 30. In this introductory chapter, I shall continue to speak of God in the context of biblical belief; in later chapters, I will make whatever qualifications are necessary.

[17] Moltmann, p. 22.

[18] Moltmann, p. 23.

[19] *Homo Viator* (New York: Harper Torchbooks, 1962), pp. 52–53.

[20] "The Theology of Hope," *Theology Digest* (February, 1968): 84.

[21] William Barrett, *Irrational Man* (Garden City, N.Y.: Doubleday Anchor Books, 1962), p. 129.

[22] Francis Fergusson observes that the notion of human life as a journey seems to be as old as the myth-making instinct itself. "All the journey metaphors are based on the analogy, which the human mind finds very natural, between physical movement and the non-spatial action of the soul" (*Dante's Drama of the Mind*, p. 4). Later, he explains "action" in these terms: "Aristotle's *action*, like Dante's *moto spiritale*, is another word for the life of the human psyche: 'Life,' says Aristotle (Butcher, *Poetics*, VI–9, p. 27), 'consists in action, and its end (goal) is a mode of action.' On this notion Aristotle built up his theory of the arts as 'imitations' of action, in their various media, and in various ways—imitations, not of the literal surfaces of life, but of the underlying movement of spirit" (p. 92).

II. KING LEAR

I

A set piece in Madeleine L'Engle's novel *The Love Letters* explains what has gone before and theorizes on what will follow. According to James G. Murray, it offers a reasonably accurate analysis of what Bach does in a two-part invention:

> Bach is saying something important, and he is saying this one important thing in two clear and separate ways, and you must keep them clear and separate, at the same time that you must know that they are uttering the same cry. And with Bach . . . it is always a cry of affirmation, of passionate affirmation.[1]

Murray admires the author's attempt to compose literature along musical lines, but feels that she does not succeed. It is his opinion that no one has ever succeeded in that attempt. When I read his comment I thought immediately of *King Lear.* Perhaps I should have taken the thought no further, for in scope it is not to Bach's two-part inventions that one compares *King Lear* but to his *St. Matthew Passion.* Nevertheless, as L'Engle observes of the two-part inventions, in *King Lear* Shakespeare "is saying something important, and he is saying this one important thing in two clear and separate ways, and you must keep them clear and separate, at the same time that you must know that they are uttering the same cry." Though the statement needs to be qualified, it can be said that Lear and

Gloucester utter the same cry. Whether or not it is a cry of "passionate affirmation" is another question. With regard to Lear alone, there are those who say yes and those who say no.

Lear cries out over the dead Cordelia:

> Why should a dog, a horse, a rat, have life,
> And thou no breath at all? Thou'lt come no more,
> Never, never, never, never, never.
>
> (V,3,308–10)[2]

But the last words he utters are these:

> Do you see this? Look on her. Look, her lips,
> Look there, look there.
>
> (V,3,312–13)

Commenting on these lines, A. C. Bradley declares that "it seems almost beyond question that any actor is false to the text who does not attempt to express, in Lear's last accent and gestures and look, an unbearable joy."[3] According to Harold Goddard, it was precisely "to make the old king's dying assertion incontrovertible" that Shakespeare permeated his play with the theme of vision.[4] Theodore Spencer implies the same thing when he says that "life is the reality under the appearance," and for Lear "the reality is *good*—it is this that breaks his heart at last."[5]

On the other side, J. K. Walton argues that "if we take it that Lear finally believes that Cordelia is alive, we alter the direction of the whole movement which has been taking place throughout the play, a movement by which he attains to an ever greater consciousness."[6] G. B. Harrison is adamant: "There is no joy in this play."[7] And Jan Kott compares it to Samuel Beckett's *Endgame* for the "tragic mockery" it makes "of the gods and the good nature, of man made in 'image and likeness.' "[8]

What is there in the play to account for this division of opinion? A silence, out of which every word emerges and against which every word resounds. Call it the silence of the gods, of the earth and sky—or, with Pascal, "the frightening silence of those infinite spaces." Perhaps what we interpret is that silence and not the play. And we interpret it according to our own life-experience. At this point a cry might be raised against interpretation. But there is room here for a kind of interpretation that will respect the silence and thereby allow the play to speak. Lear's "journey," to use Kent's word (V,3,323), ends in the silence of death. So does Gloucester's "pilgrimage" (Edgar's word, V,3,198). We must follow both along their separate ways to see how, in the gathering silence, they utter the same cry.

II

Gloucester's bastard son Edmund finds it all too easy to trick his brother Edgar out of his inheritance:

> . . . a brother noble,
> Whose nature is so far from doing harms
> That he suspects none . . .
>
> (I,2,192–94)

A forged letter is all it takes to convince his "credulous father" that Edgar is plotting against his life. It is as if Gloucester has been waiting all along for some excuse to prefer Edmund to Edgar, who, even though legitimate, was "no dearer" to him than Edmund. The thought suggests itself that, like Henry IV, who saw braver mettle in Hotspur than in his own Prince Hal, Gloucester wished secretly that "some night-tripping fairy" had exchanged the true son for the baseborn. Or like the blind Isaac, who preferred Esau the hunter to Jacob the "man of peace," even though Esau had sold his birthright for a mess of potage and had married pagan wives. He protests, of course, that he loved Edgar most "tenderly and entirely," but he has yet to learn what it is to love. It does not occur to him to assign any responsibility to himself for the "bond cracked 'twixt son and father"; he resorts rather to the "late eclipses in the sun and moon" for explanation.

Edmund knows better:

> This is the excellent foppery of the world, that when we are sick in fortune, often the surfeits of our own behavior, we make guilty of our disasters the sun, the moon, and stars; as if we were villains on necessity; fools by heavenly compulsion . . .
>
> (I,2,128–33)

In rejecting such "foppery," Edmund implies a causal relationship between sin and misfortune, from his own cynical point of view. It is "often" so, he says; but the human tendency to make it absolute is persistent—even when the evil seems out of all proportion to any guilt that might have been incurred, even when the victim protests his innocence, as in the case of Job. When Gloucester has his eyes gouged out for befriending the king and his cause, he discovers that it was Edmund who betrayed him; but, unlike Job, he is not innocent and now he knows it in his heart:

> O my follies! Then Edgar was abused.
> Kind gods, forgive me that, and prosper him.
>
> (III,7,92–93)

Nevertheless, there is a sense of evil here that is out of all proportion to Gloucester's guilt: Evil is thick in the air, something gone wild, a hideous force, by no means a mere effect.

"Why is this man blind?" Jesus' disciples asked him.

"Was he guilty of sin, or were his parents guilty?" "Neither," Jesus answered. "Rather, it was to let God's work be revealed in him" (John 9:3). The disciples asked about the cause of the man's blindness, but Jesus answered in terms of purpose.[9] Once given the blindness, how shall it serve? The story that follows tells how a man who sat in darkness was brought to see the light—physically, but more to the point, spiritually. It also tells how those who thought they saw, the Pharisees, were blinding themselves to the light and plunging into darkness.

> If only you *were* blind,
> then you would not be guilty of sin.
> But now that you claim to see,
> your sin remains.
>
> (John 9:40)

Gloucester's blindness is the beginning of light:

> I stumbled when I saw.
>
> (IV,1,19)

But those who conspired to blind him (Edmund, Cornwall, Regan and Goneril) plunge into deeper darkness because they claim to see. Like the Pharisees, they can learn nothing from interrogating the accused because they claim to know everything already. Says Regan to Gloucester:

> Be simple-answered, for we know the truth.
>
> (III,7,44)

In counterpoint "to the paradox of the blinded Gloucester who has insight," we get "the paradox of blindness in those who see too well."[10]

Gloucester is thrust out of the gates to "smell his

way to Dover." He meets his own son Edgar, who does not reveal himself but resumes the mask of madness by which he has so far "escaped the hunt." Gloucester begs Edgar to take him to the cliffs where he can plunge down into the depths of his despair and finish what the gods have begun:

> As flies to wanton boys, are we to th' gods,
> They kill us for their sport.
>
> (IV,1,36)

And so begins the pilgrimage of the pretended madman and the maddened blind man. Near Dover, on a level path, Edgar persuades his father that they are actually climbing steep ground. Gloucester is ripe for illusion (if we are willing to take Marshall McLuhan's word for it) because, having lost his sight, his power of visualization is now quite separate from his other senses. In *King Lear,* "the anguish of the third dimension is given its first verbal manifestation."[11] Standing in the middle of a plain, Edgar directs Gloucester's "gaze" to and through five two-dimensional panels, one behind the other:

> How fearful
> And dizzy 'tis to cast one's eyes so low!
> The crows and choughs that wing the midway air
> Show scarce so gross as beetles. Halfway down
> Hangs one that gathers sampire, dreadful trade!
> Methinks he seems no bigger than his head.
> The fishermen that walk upon the beach
> Appear like mice; and yond tall anchoring bark
> Diminished to her cock; her cock, a buoy
> Almost too small for sight. The murmuring surge,
> That on th' unnumb'red idle pebbles chafes,
> Cannot be heard so high. I'll look no more,
> Lest my brain turn, and the deficient sight
> Topple down headlong.
>
> (IV,6,11–24)

Then Edgar sets him "within a foot / Of th' extreme verge," and stands apart. Gloucester kneels and pours out his despair:

> O you mighty gods!
> This world I do renounce, and in your sights
> Shake patiently my great affliction off:
> If I could bear it longer and not fall
> To quarrel with your great opposeless wills,
> My snuff and loathèd part of nature should
> Burn itself out. If Edgar live, O bless him!
> (IV,6,34–40)

Then he throws himself forward. To the blind there are no degrees of darkness: The first layer is already the ultimate. When Gloucester "revives," he may, for all he knows, have struck his head on the first tumble and plunged the rest of the way unconscious.

> GLOUCESTER: Have I fall'n, or no?
> EDGAR: From the dread summit of this chalky bourn.
> Look up a-height; the shrill-gorged lark so far
> Cannot be seen or heard: do but look up.
> (IV,6,56–59)

But we know that the "dread summit" is no higher than the modest mound of his own dignity, that he falls, dignity and all, no lower than the level of his feet.

Instead of spilling his life on the rocks below, renouncing the world in the face of the mighty gods, Gloucester merely "takes a spill." The tragedy of noble sacrifice collapses into what G. Wilson Knight calls "the comedy of the grotesque."[12] Kott makes much of this collapse.[13] In his view, the gods, and the whole moral order, collapse with it. Gloucester's suicide is "a protest against undeserved suffering and the world's injustice," but only if the gods, and the whole moral order they impose, exist.

Since they do not, Gloucester's suicide solves nothing. It is only "a somersault on an empty stage." The whole situation, then, becomes grotesque.

But if the gods do not exist, Gloucester and Edgar are quite unaware of their demise.

> GLOUCESTER: You ever-gentle gods . . .
> Let not my worser spirit tempt me again
> To die before you please.
> EDGAR: Well pray you, father.
> (IV,6,219–22)

Sentiments of this sort do not fit into Kott's thesis, unless he inserts before every one of them the stage direction "cruel and mocking." But to ignore these sentiments is to fail to see what has actually taken place in this boldly imaginative scene. Edgar tells us that he "trifles" with his father's despair in order to cure it. Gloucester is a man who has ceased to wish for anything in this world; he renounces it, as he declares in the passage already quoted, because he can no longer bear it. When he ceases to wish, he ceases to hope. Somehow he must be helped to wish again. William F. Lynch maintains that "the best and the most human part of man is the ability to wish," that "one of the most splendid qualities of the outside world, whether that world be things or God or a teacher or a parent or a doctor, is the ability to communicate help in such a way as to create in others the interior ability to really wish."[14] Edgar helps his father under more than one guise, but ultimately it is as the instrument of the "clearest gods" (73):

> GLOUCESTER: Now, good sir, what are you?
> EDGAR: A most poor man, made tame to fortune's blows;
> Who, by the art of known and feeling sorrows,
> Am pregnant to good pity. Give me your hand,

I'll lead you to some biding.
GLOUCESTER: Hearty thanks;
The bounty and the benison of heaven
To boot, and boot.

(IV,6,223–28)

To give another man one's hand, in trust, is truly to wish again. And to wish is to hope.

III

It is right after his suicide attempt that Gloucester's path crosses Lear's. "Enter Lear, fantastically dressed in wild flowers." So runs the eighteenth-century stage direction found in modern editions. With Edgar we cry out:

O thou side-piercing sight!

(IV,6,85)

But first, like Kent, we must follow Lear on his journey from the beginning.

It is the king's desire to shake off all cares and "unburthened crawl toward death" (I,1,43). But now his burdens begin. He demands to be loved; he asks for great wings of love to gather him in whenever he wishes to pause. Goneril and Regan know how to spread their wings in words, but Cordelia, of whom most is expected, knows that her love is too "ponderous" for flight. She even dares to say that when she weds, her husband shall carry half her love with him. To a man in love with Love this is intolerable, and Lear becomes the victim of his own absolutizing imagination. Through the magnifying glass of such an imagination reality loses its true perspective and its true edges. As Lynch says:

> The good becomes the tremendously good, the evil becomes the absolutely evil, the grey becomes the black or white, the complicated, because it is difficult to handle, becomes, in desperation, the completely simple. . . . But above all, everything assumes a greater weight than it has, and becomes a greater burden.[15]

Lear disowns Cordelia, banishes Kent for taking her part, and bids Cornwall and Albany, with his two daughters' dowers, to "digest the third." "Unburthened" thus, he is stripped for the journey.

As Heilman has pointed out, it is virtually a commonplace to regard Lear's journey as purgatorial in nature.[16] But in what sense is this so? In attempting to answer, I lean again on Lynch's study of the imagination as healer of the hopeless. Lear's journey can be said to begin in "the nightmare world of unqualified, absolute feelings" and to end in "the valley of the human."[17] But the valley is ringed with fire.

> To move through the fire into the valley of the human is to move right through a whole camp of these absolutes. Everything the self turns to for salvation actually dissolves and gives no grip upon itself. Everything is at first a fire, yet it turns out to be not fire but balm. The whole question is, how can that be? To give up an "absolute," to give up a "necessity," to give up that with which one is absolutely identified, to give up what was a point of absolute security, to give up a black-and-white world—each of the surrenders is a trial by fire. But each turns out to be a balm because these things were weights that burdened us and brought no taste of freedom.

For Lear the "absolute" is inevitably bound up with his kingship. He identifies so completely with his role as king that he cannot relinquish the title.

> . . . we shall retain
> The name, and all th' addition to a king.
> (I,1,137–38)

He lives in a black-and-white world of king and subject, and woe to those who think otherwise. To Oswald, Goneril's steward, he shouts:

> O, you, sir, you! Come you hither, sir. Who am I, sir?
> OSWALD: My lady's father.
> LEAR: "My lady's father"? My lord's knave, you whoreson dog, you slave, you cur!
>
> (I,4,79–82)

Since Cordelia loves him only according to her bond, "no more no less," and not as befits his majesty, her love cannot be love at all, and he responds in kind. To the king of France he says of her:

> I would not from your love make such a stray
> To match you where I hate. . . .
>
> (I,1,211–12)

But now he finds the self-enclosed circle of his majesty, the absolutized base of all his feeling and thinking and center of his hopes, breaking up. He wanted to be independent, and to that end he kept a hundred knights, but his daughters tug at him mercilessly:

> GONERIL: Hear me, my lord.
> What need you five-and-twenty? ten? or five?
> To follow in a house where twice so many
> Have a command to tend you?
> REGAN: What need one?
> LEAR: O reason not the need!
>
> (II,4,259–63)

Uncertain of his position, he finds that he is too aggressive. When he calls upon the "nimble lightnings" to dart their blinding flames into Goneril's "scornful eyes," Regan cries out:

O the blest gods!
So will you wish on me when the rash mood is on.
LEAR: No, Regan, thou shalt never have my curse.
(II,4,167–69)

But when she joins forces with Goneril, he is afraid of not being aggressive enough. To the gods he prays:

If it be you that stirs these daughters' hearts
Against their father, fool me not so much
To bear it tamely; touch me with noble anger,
And let not women's weapons, water drops,
Stain my man's cheeks.
(II,4,273–77)

He wants love and he finds hate, in himself as well as in others. He had such "reasonable" hopes, and now he faces hopelessness:

O Fool, I shall go mad!
(II,4,285)

When all the idols surrounding his majesty are dethroned, he will declare:

. . . they told me I was everything; 'tis a lie, I am not ague-proof.
(IV,6,106)

He is now in the heart of the fire, "bound / Upon a wheel of fire" (IV,7,47), and there is chaos within and without. It is at this point that he meets the blind Gloucester, who cries out:

O ruined piece of nature!
(IV,6,136)

But now Cordelia, arrived from France, sends her gentlemen to gather him up. When he wakes, he says:

> Where have I been? Where am I?
>
> (IV,7,52)

He is in the valley of the human. Later, he recognizes Cordelia, and love is recognized for what it is. With much greater truth he can now "unburthened crawl toward death." Even when Edmund takes them prisoner, he can say to Cordelia:

> Come, let's away to prison:
> We two alone will sing like birds i' th' cage:
> When thou dost ask me blessing, I'll kneel down
> And ask of thee forgiveness: so we'll live,
> And pray, and sing, and tell old tales, and laugh
> At gilded butterflies, and hear poor rogues
> Talk of court news; and we'll talk with them too,
> Who loses and who wins, who's in, who's out;
> And take upon's the mystery of things,
> As if we were God's spies. . . .
>
> (V,3,8–17)

IV

Having passed through the fire, Lear has reached the valley of the human, carried there on the wings of love and compassion. But his journey is not over. Within the valley a final road must be taken and Lear knows it leads to death.

But Cordelia arrives before him, and that he did not know:

> And my poor fool is hanged: no, no, no life?
> Why should a dog, a horse, a rat, have life,

And thou no breath at all? Thou'lt come no more,
Never, never, never, never, never.

(V,3,307–10)

It is "as though the whole play in anguish brings to birth one transcendent loveliness," says Knight, "only to stamp it out, kill it."[18] Is death a judgment? On whom? Why is the flower trampled in full bloom?

Men must endure
Their going hence, even as their coming hither:
Ripeness is all.

(V,2,9–11)

But why is man born in the first place if he comes into the world only to die? And why is one man born blind? And another made blind? And why should man ever see anything if in the end he is to see nothing?

The world is filled with a great silence, and against this silence both Lear and Gloucester utter the same cry. Lear's cry circles the globe, a great question hanging unanswered across the sky. Gloucester's cry loses some of its power to disturb us because at the end a note of joy unmistakably chimes in. When Edgar reveals himself to him,

. . . his flawed heart—
Alack, too weak the conflict to support—
Twixt two extremes of passion, joy and grief,
Burst smilingly.

(V,3,198–200)

Edgar lives, but Cordelia is dead. There are some who wish to say that Lear, too, died with joy in his heart, even if that joy originated in hallucination:

Do you see this? Look on her. Look, her lips,
Look there, look there.

(V,3,312–13)

But the point is that at the moment of death such joy, no matter what its origin, is only tangential to the main question posed by Gloucester's "pilgrimage" and Lear's "journey." What is the meaning of man, if he is born only to suffer and die? That is the play's question.

Cordelia's death makes the question agonizingly acute. Lear and Gloucester are old; they have suffered much.

> He hates him
> That would upon the rack of this tough world
> Stretch him out longer.
>
> (V,3,315–17)

When Cornwall, Goneril and Regan die, we do not argue with Albany's reaction:

> The judgment of the heavens, that makes us tremble,
> Touches us not with pity.
>
> (V,3,233–34)

Edmund's death may well have moved us, had the play's main thrust been his; for before he dies, he begins to see (V,3,245). But when we learn of his death, following upon Cordelia's, we are inclined to say with Albany:

> That's but a trifle here.
>
> (V,3,297)

It is Cordelia's death, and the fact that Lear must bear it, that shakes us to the depths.

Why? Because she is innocent. Because she is good. Because she deserved to live. Because Lear, who has suffered so much, deserved to live for a time in joyful conversation with her. Why so much undeserved suffering? Why this sudden upset of what seemed so careful a balance of the scales of justice?

In raising such questions, the tragedy of *King Lear*

has been likened to the Book of Job. But as we indicated earlier in discussing the Gloucester-theme, the starting-point is different. Job is innocent; at least there is no question of the existence of the kind of sin for which his suffering might be seen to be the consequence. For Lear there is. While ultimately he is "a man more sinned against than sinning" (III,2,59), the question of his own culpability in the matter must not be overlooked.

McLuhan observes that it was some time after printing that authors began to discover "points of view." In the first age of print they were "led to adopt in varying degrees the only available soothsayer mask, that of the medieval clown."[19] This observation is supported by Enid Welford's study of the Fool in literary history: In *King Lear* Shakespeare makes use of the conventions of "fool-literature," which were used "as the vehicle for a reasoned criticism of life."[20] With this function of the Fool in mind, we note how the Fool's very presence was a reminder to Lear of how he had sinned against his own daughter:

LEAR: . . . Where's my Fool? I have not seen him this two days.
KNIGHT: Since my young lady's going into France, sir, the Fool hath much pined away.
LEAR: No more of that; I have noted it well.

(I,4,72–76)

Later, in the Fool's presence, a sentence escapes Lear's lips that tells us unmistakably where his mind is:

I did her wrong—

(I,5,24)

Nor is he ever allowed to forget that it is he who "has made Goneril and Regan efficacious in the world; they are projections of his own divided nature."[21] And of his own divided kingdom:

FOOL: . . . Nuncle, give me an egg, and I'll give thee two crowns.
LEAR: What two crowns shall they be?
FOOL: Why, after I have cut the egg i' th' middle and eat up the meat, the two crowns of the egg. When thou clovest thy crown i' th' middle and gav'st away both parts, thou bor'st thine ass on thy back o'er the dirt. Thou hadst little wit in thy bald crown when thou gav'st thy golden one away.

(I,4,159–67)

The Fool is never heard of again after the third act; but toward the end of that act, as if to prepare for his absence, he announces to Lear the presence of another "fool," the disguised Edgar, to whom Lear will attach himself as "my philosopher" (III,4,179). And it is Edgar who takes up the Fool's point of view with regard to the inevitable consequences of sinful folly. After his victory over Edmund, he says (in so didactic a fashion that we seem to hear the playwright speaking):

> The gods are just, and of our pleasant vices
> Make instruments to plague us:
> The dark and vicious place where thee he [Gloucester] got
> Cost him his eyes.

(V,3,172–74)

And Edmund, who early in the play recognized "the excellent foppery" of the world in making the sun and the moon and the stars responsible for the evils men bring upon themselves, is quite in accord with Edgar's point of view:

> Th' hast spoken right; 'tis true.

(V,3,175)

To assert some connection between what men do and what happens to them by way of misfortune is not to teach that every misfortune is traceable to some personal sin. It explains, to some extent, the presence of evil in the world, but it leaves untouched the mystery of undeserved suffering, evoked so powerfully in the last scene of the play: What is the meaning of man, if he is born only to suffer and die?

"One morning," wrote Albert Camus, "after many dark nights of despair, an irrepressible longing to live will announce to us the fact all is finished and that suffering has no more meaning than happiness."[22] Was this Lear's experience? "Lear and Gloucester," says Kott, "are adherents of eschatology; they desperately believe in the existence of absolutes." Like Job, "they invoke the gods, believe in justice, appeal to laws of nature." But the play, he maintains, "makes a tragic mockery of all eschatologies."[23] In the end, for Kott, Lear utters the same cry as Hamm in *Endgame*. It is not at all clear that this is so. Once, in Beckett's play, Hamm calls upon God. To Clov and Nagg he says:

Let us pray to God.
NAGG: *(clasping his hands, closing his eyes, in a gabble)* Our Father which art—
HAMM: Silence! In silence! Where are your manners? *(Pause)* Off we go. *(Attitudes of prayer. Silence. Abandoning his attitude, discouraged)* Well?
CLOV: *(abandoning his attitude)* What a hope! And you?
HAMM: Sweet damn all! (*To* NAGG) And you?
NAGG: Wait! *(Pause. Abandoning his attitude)* Nothing doing!
HAMM: The bastard! He doesn't exist.

There is no denying that this dialogue is rooted in human experience. But it is not the experience of Lear. Nowhere does Lear say that the gods do not exist, that "suffering has no more meaning than happiness," that everything is absurd. At the beginning of the play we see him absolutize his need to love and at the end of the play we see him cured. There is nothing to make us think that now at the end he absolutizes his need to know. This is what Hamm does in *Endgame*. He erases the mystery of the universe in a single breath: "The bastard! He doesn't exist." The need to know is absolutized into the need for certainty in everything. There is no room for faith as a way of knowing. "Religious faith," says William Lynch, "has always taught man not only to know, but to be able to live in waiting, in a kind of darkness, making war on the desire of man to reduce the whole of reality, supernatural and natural, to his own limited ways of knowing."[24] In *King Lear* the possibility of religious faith is left open.[25]

Lear and Gloucester, then, utter the same cry. It is not the same cry as Hamm's, but the silence is the same, the silence against which it is uttered. Is it a cry of "passionate affirmation"? It does not affirm with certainty the final meaning of man, but it affirms passionately the spirit of man who carries his search even into the gates of death. Lear is a pilgrim to the very end. If his cry is a cry of despair, it is the kind of despair that expresses the essential hunger of his being, that defines the human nature he shares with all men by its openness to become what of himself he has no power to be. To be like God was man's first temptation (Genesis 2:5); but if man's nature is not ultimately meaningless, to be like God is his only fulfillment (Apoc. 2:7).

> Vex not his ghost: O, let him pass!
>
> (V,3,314)

NOTES

[1] *The Critic* (February–March, 1967): 82.

[2] Line references are to The Signet Classic Shakespeare: *King Lear,* ed. Russell Fraser. Copyright © 1963 by Russell Fraser. By arrangement with The New American Library, Inc., New York, N.Y.

[3] *Shakespearean Tragedy* (London: Macmillan & Co., 1904; New York: St. Martin's Press, 1905), p. 291.

[4] *The Meaning of Shakespeare* (Chicago: University of Chicago Press, Phoenix Books, 1960), Vol. 2, p. 163.

[5] *Shakespeare and the Nature of Man,* 2nd ed. (New York: Macmillan Co., 1949), p. 152.

[6] Quoted in an additional note in *The Arden Shakespeare: King Lear,* ed. Kenneth Muir (New York: Barnes & Noble, 1961), p. 259.

[7] *Shakespeare's Tragedies* (London: Routledge & Kegan Paul, 1951; New York: Oxford University Press, 1969), p. 183.

[8] *Shakespeare Our Contemporary* (Garden City, N.Y.: Doubleday Anchor Books, 1966), p. 147.

[9] *The Anchor Bible, The Gospel According to John,* I–XII, trans. with an introduction and notes by Raymond E. Brown (Garden City, N.Y.: Doubleday & Co., 1966), p. 369.

[10] Robert B. Heilman, *This Great Stage* (Baton Rouge: Louisiana State University Press, 1948), p. 59.

[11] *The Gutenberg Galaxy* (Toronto: University of Toronto Press, 1965), p. 16.

[12] *The Wheel of Fire,* 4th ed. (London: Methuen & Co., 1949), p. 171.

[13] *Shakespeare Our Contemporary,* p. 147.

[14] William F. Lynch, S.J., *Images of Hope* (New York: Mentor-Omega Books, 1966), p. 135.

[15] *Images of Hope,* p. 91.

[16] *This Great Stage,* p. 91.

[17] *Images of Hope,* p. 101.

[18] *The Wheel of Fire,* p. 204.

[19] *The Gutenberg Galaxy,* p. 136.

[20] *The Fool: His Social and Literary History* (Gloucester, Mass.: Peter Smith, 1966).

[21] Heilman, "Tragedy and Melodrama," in *Texas Quarterly* (Summer, 1960): 43.

[22] *The Rebel* (New York: Vintage, 1956), p. 261.

[23] *Shakespeare Our Contemporary,* pp. 166, 147.

[24] *Images of Hope,* p. 98.

[25] This possibility is categorically denied in a book entitled *King Lear and the Gods,* published by The Huntington Library in

1966 but not brought to my attention until a review of it appeared in *The Shakespeare Quarterly* (Winter, 1969). The author, William R. Elton, argues that Lear moves from pagan belief to disbelief: The direction of the tragedy is toward an "annihilation of faith in divine justice" (p. 334). Elton supports his conclusion by comparing the play to Sir Philip Sidney's *Arcadia* (1590), a major source, and by contrasting it to the old *King Leir*, a probable source play, and providing as a context a wide-ranging investigation of contemporary writings. But, like Kott's, his conclusion goes too far. There is nothing in the text of *King Lear* to make us conclude that Lear, at the end, has absolutized his need to know. In one section of his study, Elton gives an enlightening exegesis of "taking upon oneself the mystery of things": In Renaissance religious terms the idea contains "presumptuous or blasphemous overtones" (p. 250). But the very writing of the play, and our viewing of it, is nothing other than taking upon ourselves the mystery of things. The mystery of things, to the very end, defies every attempt to "comprehend" it, to reduce it to categories of pure reason and "divine justice" (a point I shall pursue further in Chapter VIII).

III. THE ROAD TO DAMASCUS

"I dream; therefore I exist." That is Strindberg's variation of the Cartesian formula.[1] In *Till Damaskus,* his trilogy of dramatic inquiry into the meaning of existence, he seeks "to reproduce the disconnected but apparently logical form of a dream." The characters "double and multiply; they evaporate, crystallise, scatter and converge. But a single consciousness holds sway over all—that of the dreamer."[2] The dreamer is called the Stranger (*den okände,* "the Unknown"), and Strindberg creates him in his own image. The dream he dreams is a restless journey of the mind.

The Road to Damascus has been carefully raked by critics for its autobiographical elements.[3] The dream form that dictates its methods has been recognized and analyzed.[4] So has the more important form, that of a journey. But the exact nature of the Stranger's spiritual journey, which is, after all, the life of the play, has not been sufficiently explored. It is this spiritual journey that I shall try to follow.

Since the Stranger's journey involves conversion from one form of life to another, Strindberg compares it to Saul's journey to Damascus. Like Saul, the Stranger was "breathing threats" against "the followers of the Way" (Acts 9:1,2). Like Saul, he becomes aware of "all the harm he has been doing" (9:14). The Stranger's Ananias is the Confessor, through whom the Unseen One will show him "how much he himself must suffer" (9:16). Suffering becomes the way to knowledge, "as though scales fell away from [his] eyes" (9:18). But not all at once. Each part of the trilogy, as Raymond Williams shows, "ends with the Stranger's conversion but the Second and Third Parts begin again with his unbelief; the conversion at the end of each part increases in conviction until at the end of the play it is final."[5]

There is a different quality to each stage of the Stranger's conversion. To appreciate this we can do nothing better than to follow his conversion according to the classic formula, in the words of St. Bonaventure, of "the journey of the soul to God" *(Itinerarium mentis in Deum)*. The *Itinerarium* has been used to show what Dante was up to in *Vita Nuova* and in the *Purgatorio*.[6] In view of Strindberg's indebtedness to Dante for both structure and theme, it is not surprising to find that Bonaventure's formula works equally well for *The Road to Damascus.*

There are three successive directions in which the soul's love (or desire) moves in its search for God: *extra nos, intra nos* and *super nos.* Moving in the first direction, the pilgrim looks "naïvely outward *(extra nos)* as a child does, at the delights and perils of the world around him." Then he "looks inward *(intra nos)* endeavoring to understand the sufferings and the true or illusory objects of his own psyche." Finally, he "turns outward again, but all that he sees . . . are signs and figures pointing upward *(super nos)*" to Someone or Something beyond himself.[7]

These three directions describe the soul's main thrust at successive stages of its life, but one direction need not end before the pull of the other two begins. (In fact, it would be possible to find traces of all three directions in almost every scene.) In Part I of Strindberg's trilogy, the main thrust is *extra nos:* The Stranger looks naïvely outward, but the labyrinth of his psyche is already forming and the "signs and figures" are pointing. In the second part, the Stranger primarily looks inward *(intra nos)* and in the third, upward *(super nos)*.

To Damascus, Part I

At the very outset of his journey, the Stranger is standing on a street corner, waiting. He moves from the street corner through seven "stations" to the Asylum, then returns to the street corner, moving through the same seven stations in reverse order. What is he waiting for? That is the question he is asked by the Lady, whom he meets on the corner. He answers:

> If only I knew . . . For forty years I've been waiting for something. Luck, I believe it's called [*lyckan,* happiness, good fortune]. Or at least the end of bad luck.[8] (I,1,i)

With these words, the action of the play, the purpose of the journey, is projected: to go in search of what he has been waiting for.[9]

At the outset, he is looking outward: Actually, he says, he is waiting for the post office to open; there's a letter there that has been forwarded from place to place without catching up with him. But when the time comes to pick it up, he holds back. He is afraid it will be bad news: It will not contain the money in payment for royalties from his writings; more likely it will be the court order summoning him to answer for the charge of tax evasion. This has always been his experience: "Whenever the golden fruit fell into my hands, it turned out to be poisoned or rotten inside" (I,1,i). It is typical of the Stranger's frame of mind that in looking "naïvely outward" for the object of his search, he will see both delight and peril in the same object. Such an expectation is not without basis in reality, but for the Stranger it creates an ambivalence of crippling proportions. It is as if, like Adam, he had broken out of time by snatching the golden fruit before God was ready to give it. Now, he breaks out of time by stepping back, afraid to put out his hand, only to discover later that "the time of his visitation" has passed him by. This he recognizes as his original sin: "I didn't want to be made a fool of" (I,l,i; 5,ii). Lear might have said the same thing. But the Lady warns the Stranger that he cannot "escape his destiny." And visibly, even if obliquely, she keeps reminding him of it by her crocheting, like one of the three Fates spinning her web (I,2,iv).[10]

The Lady, too, is seen by the Stranger as an object fraught with both delight and peril: "You were sent here either to save me or destroy me" (I,1,i). He calls her Eve. He never really manages to convince himself that she, too, is a person in search of salvation. Even though she calls him her "liberator" (by marrying her, he will liberate her from the "werewolf," her husband), she is regarded primarily as the means of *his* redemption.

> I once thought my redemption was at hand. Through a woman. Seventh heaven. What a delusion! It was the beginning of the seventh hell. (I,1,i)

But when the Lady kisses him, he is willing to try again, and he follows her to her home, where she still lives with her husband, the Doctor.

The "werewolf" is surely one of the greater perils that stand in his way to happiness. To the Lady the Stranger cries:

> I'm suffocating here! I can't sleep a night in this house. He

actually looks like a werewolf, and when he's around, you turn into a pillar of salt. (I,1,ii)

The Doctor has become a werewolf because he lost faith in God's justice when he was blamed as a child for a prank the Stranger had played. The Stranger's sins, like a mill, "keep grinding the past" (II,4,ii). Earlier he had seen himself in the corpse of a man who had drunk himself to death, in a beggar looking in gutters for the "golden ring" he had thrown away, in a mental patient whom the Doctor had nicknamed "Caesar."

Why does everything have to keep coming back again and again? Corpses and beggars and fools and madmen and whole lives and childhood memories. (I,1,ii)

He begs the Lady to leave the werewolf and go away with him. That is exactly what she wants, and so they run off and get married.

A few days of happiness, but out of the happiness, as if by spontaneous generation, come the maggots of sorrow. "I just feel that happiness cannot be part of my life" (I,2,ii). And yet he goes on searching.[11] Still looking naïvely outward, he places a fantastic hope in money. He can endure anything "except this deadly poverty" which forces them "to run the gauntlet of bellboys and waiters and doormen and room clerks." The Lady mocks him for "the free and happy life" he has given her. But one day, triumphant, he shows her a registered letter, unopened.

THE LADY: The money!
THE STRANGER: Came this morning! Who can destroy me now?
THE LADY: Don't! You know who can hurt us.
THE STRANGER: And who might that be?
THE LADY: "A haughty spirit goeth before a fall."—Remember?
THE STRANGER: It isn't the haughtiness, it's the spirit the gods can't stand! (I,2,ii)

But when he opens the letter, there is no money, only a royalty statement showing that he has nothing coming from his writings. He throws the letter up in the air, and hurls his challenge:

> Strike me with your lightning—if you dare! . . . Who are you who dare to wake me from my dream of love? To snatch the cup from my lips and the woman from my arms? What's the matter, are you jealous, you gods or devils? (I,2,ii)

Poverty forces them to seek shelter with the Lady's parents in the mountains. "Another lion's den, one more snake pit?" the Stranger asks. The Old Man gives them a grudging welcome:

> I won't wish you happiness—it doesn't exist; but I will wish you the strength to bear your fate. (I,2,v)

Although the Mother is at first more friendly, for the Stranger she turns out to be the snake in the pit. One day, in the rose room, she tempts his wife to read the book he wrote about his first marriage—a book so black and bitter that he had made the Lady promise never to read it. When he enters the room, the "smell of a crushed snake" is still hovering in the air and the Lady has broken her promise. Full of the poison that he himself had prepared, she says:

> I feel as if I'd eaten of the tree of knowledge. My eyes have been opened, and I know the difference between good and evil. I didn't before. Now I see what an evil man you really are, and I know why you wanted to call me Eve. (I,3,i)

The Stranger feels himself cursed again by his own past. "Everything has to come back, repeat itself, everything—little schoolboy tricks and big manly crimes." Unable to remain in the Lady's sight, he flees the house.

Three months later he comes to his senses in an asylum, the cloister of "The Good Help." The Abbess in charge tells him that he was seen in the mountains above the ravine, challenging the clouds with a cross that he had torn down from a wayside calvary; that he fell over the cliff and was found there, uninjured but delirious, complaining, like Jacob the wrestler, of an invisible pain in his thigh. In his delirium, he reproached himself with every sin imaginable and kept seeing before his eyes all his "victims." And his "thoughts revolved mainly around money" (I,3,ii).

But the Stranger's emergence from his "feverish dreams" is itself told in the shape of a feverish dream. The cloister is peopled with the figures from his past: "Their whole appearance and all their gestures are ghostlike," the stage directions read. Here, he meets the Confessor, his Ananias, for the first time. In the black and white robes of a Dominican, the Confessor reads over him the Curse of Deuteronomy, the same curse that the werewolf used to read over him, *in absentia,* for having ruined his life. "If thou wilt not harken unto the voice of the Lord thy God . . . all these curses shall come upon thee, and overtake thee" (Deut. 28). The Stranger remembers that in the Book of Deuteronomy the Lord also promises a blessing. "Yes," says the Confessor, "to those who keep His commandments."

In a letter to a friend, Strindberg himself vividly describes what happens at the "Asylum-point." If we ignore his reference to Kierkegaard, the description is helpful.

> The trick lies in the composition, which symbolizes the "Repetition" Kierkegaard talks about. The action rolls forward to the Asylum-point, where "it kicks against the prick" and is spurred back to the beginning. A pilgrimage, a return to school, learning one's lesson for good, getting paid back in

spades. And then something new can begin where the game ends and where it began.[12]

The Stranger returns to the house in search of his wife but finds only the Mother. Again, she is an object of ambivalence for him: He finds her mean because she is "religious," but because she is religious he finds in her a mother. She begs God to have mercy on him and pleads with the Stranger to go on his knees before the Crucified, for only He can undo the past.

My son: you have left Jerusalem and you are on the way to Damascus. Go there. The same way you came here. And plant a cross at each station, but stop at the seventh. You don't have fourteen, as He had. (I,3,iv)

"Longing for the light," the Stranger retraces his steps, and tries to make up for the wrongs he has done—to the Beggar, to the Doctor, to the Lady—making, as it were, the Stations of the Cross. He doesn't believe that Christ could suffer for him; he must himself suffer.[13] And things begin to go well for him (I,4,iii). God, it seems, has accepted his atonement. At the street corner where he first met the Lady, he is reunited to her. In the post office, the letter he left unopened is still waiting. It contains the money! "I didn't want to be made a fool of by life," he says. "And so I was" (I,5,ii). The Lady begs him to go into the church with her.

THE STRANGER: Oh, well, I can always pass through. But as for staying there—definitely not.
THE LADY: How do you know? . . . Come on. . . . You'll get to hear new songs in there.
THE STRANGER: *(following her toward the church door)* Maybe. Maybe.
THE LADY: Come! (I,5,ii)

In the journey of his mind to God, the Stranger has persistently looked naïvely outward *(extra nos)*. But in "making the seven stations," he has already begun to turn his gaze inward *(intra nos)*, endeavoring to understand his sufferings and the true and illusory objects of his psyche. This endeavor will intensify in *To Damascus*, Part II, and will become its main thrust.

To Damascus, Part II

The question of suffering is posed very early in the Stranger's journey. It is, in a sense, his "bad luck" that sets him going. After his marriage to the Lady, he cries out in a moment of ecstasy:

Eve, come die with me now, Eve, this very instant, for in the next all the pain will be back with us again.
THE LADY: No, I'm not ready to die yet.
THE STRANGER: Why not?
THE LADY: I keep thinking there's still something I have to do. Perhaps I haven't suffered enough yet. . . .
THE STRANGER: Do you think that's the reason for living?
THE LADY: It seems like it. (I,2,ii)

But if suffering is the reason for living, the Lady still requires a reason for suffering, and it is the Stranger who tries to assign one. At the end of Part I, when he finds the money in the letter he left unopened, the Lady exclaims:

All our trials and tribulations, all our tears—all in vain.
THE STRANGER: Not in vain! It may look like dirty playing, but it really isn't. I wronged someone, the Unseen One, when I suspected that—
THE LADY: Sh, sh. No more of that. No accusations. (I,5,ii)

It is as if to assign such a reason is to give new cause for suffering. No matter what the cause, every new suffering raises again the question of its meaning. And a man must go within himself in an effort to understand.

In Part II, the source of his suffering is threefold. He suffers as Cain the Outcast in relation to the Doctor, the brother whom he "slew" (II,1; 2,iii). He suffers as Orestes in relation to his wife, the "fury" whose "inventive ability" for torturing him exceeds his "most infernal devices" (II,1). He suffers as Lucifer in relation to the making of gold, by means of which he shall write "the final chapter in the history of the universe" (II,2,i; 4,i). In all three relationships there is the anguished attempt to distinguish between the true and the illusory. "He believes all evil to be truth, and all good to be lies" (II,4,i).

The werewolf Doctor has gone mad, but he confronts the Stranger with a savage lucidity, confronts the schoolboy whose injustice had crushed his spirit, the "Great Genius" who had robbed him of his wife, the Liberator before whom no bond is sacred, not even the bond between father and child (for the Doctor believes that he himself is the father of the child the Lady is expecting). With some of Strindberg's most powerful language on his lips, he lays his curse upon the Stranger:

When the pendulum strikes at the hour of midnight, I shall blow my cold breath on your heart—and it will stop like a run-down clock! When you sit working, I shall come with a poppy that you cannot see, and it shall put your thoughts to sleep; it shall bring disorder and confusion to your mind and make you see visions that you will be unable to distinguish from reality! I shall lie like a rock on your path, and you will stumble—I shall be the thorn that pricks your hand as it is about to pluck the rose; my soul shall stretch and fasten itself like the web of a spider across your soul—and through the woman you stole from me, I shall lead you like a bullock; your child shall be mine, and I shall speak through its mouth—in its eyes you shall read my gaze; and so you will push the child away from you as if it were an enemy. . . . (II,1)

At a later meeting, he poisons the Stranger's mind with lies—or is it the "bitter, unvarnished truth"? He tells him that before either of them had met the Lady she was "the mistress of a married man, whom she later brought suit against for rape. She had forced herself upon him in his studio after posing for him in the nude" (II,4,i). How long must we suffer him? the Lady cries. "So long as *he* suffers and our conscience keeps flogging us . . . " (II,2,i).

At the beginning of Part II, the Stranger and the Lady have already left each other four times—each one in his turn—and each time they have returned. When the Confessor, who was the Lady's first love, asks the Mother how they are getting along now, she answers:

Half the day they get along like angels, and the rest of the day they torture each other like demons. (II,1)

The Lady herself says of her husband:

I think of him as being everything that is evil—and in the next moment, everything that is good. (II,1)

She opens all his letters because she wants to know with whom she has joined her fate (". . . he is corresponding with alchemists!"). She deceives him into wearing her former husband's clothes because it amuses her to torture and humiliate him. She leaves a purse lying around in order to see if he is a thief. When she learns of her pregnancy, she first wants to destroy the unborn child, then wants to let it live, for it will "blot out the dark past and bring us light." But before the child is born, she threatens to sue for divorce. Her threat comes to nothing. When she appears before the public prosecutor, she impulsively brings information against her former husband, the Doctor, for invasion of privacy and attempted murder. The werewolf, in his turn, brings charges against her for falsely accusing him. In order to make sure that their child will not be born in prison the Stranger takes the blame for her crime upon himself.

When the child comes, it does not bring a light bright enough to pierce their darkness. For the Stranger the darkness is made yet deeper when he learns that the children of his former marriage have a stepfather. Why do the pangs of conscience come after the act, and not before? "Can you answer that?" (II,4,ii). "It is eight thousand times," says the Chorus in a Noh play, "before regret runs in a smooth-worn groove, forestalls itself."[14]

The third, and very special, source of his suffering is his alchemy. Here, particularly, the need to distinguish between the true and the illusory is at its most anguished. In Part I, when the Stranger was still looking naively outward, he wanted gold for quite an ordinary reason: to enrich himself. "I've had everything I wished for," he says. "Unfortunately I forgot to wish for gold" (I,2,ii). But in Part II, looking inward, he wants it for very different reasons. To the Lady he declares:

> I hold the fate of the world in my crucible—and a week from now the richest of the rich will be poor. Gold, the false measuring rod of wealth, will have ceased to be the ruler—we shall all be poor—and the children of mankind will be crawling about like ants when their anthill has been trampled upon!
>
> Do you think I have been making gold for the purpose of enriching ourselves and others? Oh no! I have done it in the hope that the present world order may be done away with—may be destroyed! Don't you see? I am the devastator, the disintegrator, the one who sets the universe afire. (II,2,i)

In the first days of his marriage, this same "devastator" wanted to take all creation in his hands "and knead it into something more nearly perfect, more enduring, more beautiful" (I,2,ii). At both extremes, he has the desires of a god. Now, by his alchemy, he will work his will.[15]

In a banquet scene of great theatricality, expressive of the labyrinth in his brain through which truth and illusion trace and retrace their way, the Stranger is feted for having made the "most devastating" of all discoveries —a discovery "divined by the followers of Pythagoras, forecast and nurtured by Albertus and Paracelsus"—the making of gold. "Gentlemen," he says, "to me it has always been a cause of pride that I am not easily deceived . . ." (II,3,i). But before his very eyes the banquet scene is turned into bedlam. Caesar, the madman whose madness turns out later to be a pretense, declares that the Stranger's gold-making is nothing but "hocus-pocus," the work of "an imposter, a charlatan!" And the Beggar acquaints him with the facts:

> You, who consider yourself to be the man of the century—you accept an invitation from a society of alcoholics to have yourself feted as a man of science! (II,3,i)

And who is going to pay for the banquet? The alchemist! But "the fellow who knows how to make gold can't pay!" So they throw him into prison. Is his gold-making nothing but "a vain and horrible illusion"? It cannot be. Yet, when his wife tells him that his discovery has been confirmed in England, he refuses to believe it.

For the sake of his gold-making, he left his wife and child. Now, steeped in the shame of his failure, he cannot go back to them. "My poor liberator," the Lady says, "now you are bound hand and foot. . . ." To the Confessor, she says:

Nothing is left for this unhappy man but to leave this world behind and take refuge in a monastery.
THE CONFESSOR: So he still does not believe he is the great genius that he actually is?
THE LADY: No, he believes nothing that is good of anyone—not even of himself. . . .
THE CONFESSOR: Yes—that is the divine punishment that was meted out to him: that he believes lies to be truth, because he refused to accept the truth. (II,4,iii)

Bitter, yet hoping to emerge from the labyrinth of his fevered brain, the Stranger lets the Confessor lead him to the monastery.

To Damascus, Part III

The way to the monastery is "uphill and roundabout" (III,1). But the monastery, rising high above the treetops, is clearly in view. The Stranger exclaims:

I have never seen anything so white on this unclean earth—except in my dreams! Yes, this has been the dream of my youth: a house and home where peace and purity would dwell. . . . You pure abode, I welcome you with open arms! . . . Now I feel I have at last found my home. (III,1)

Now, at last, he is looking outward again, but what he sees are "signs and figures pointing upward *(super nos).*"

These signs have been there from the very beginning, but not always apprehended. Over and over again in Part I, and on a couple of occasions in Part II, there is the sound of Mendelssohn's *Funeral March,* "That terrible music," like the voice of Everyman's Angel of Death, "persecuting him." Over and over again there is the hunting horn, the call of the "mysterious huntsman" searching him out. When he first meets the Lady, she is wearing a Christmas rose on her breast. In days gone by, he observes, people used such roses to cure madness, and they could tell that spring was in the air when they began to wither. Suddenly, after a funeral has gone by, the Stranger is afraid—"not of death—but this other thing—the unknown." The Lady takes him by the hand, "like a good boy," as the choir in the chapel nearby salutes Mary, Star of the Sea, *Ave, Maris Stella.* In the *Salve Regina,* heard later in Part II, Mary the Queen is invoked as the hope of every exile, of every child of Eve.

It is also in Part II that the Stranger, drinking himself blind in the company of "beggars, nightwalkers and prostitutes," feels the breath of the mysterious huntsman. Clutching his breast, he cries out:

> Oh! Oh! Now he is coming nearer to me—he, the Terrible One, who sucks my heart out of my breast. . . . He is coming, the Invisible One, who has pursued me these many years. He is upon me—he is here! (II,4,i)

At that moment the Dominican priest enters, carrying to the bedside of a dying man the sacrament of the living bread.[16] They all start to "howl like savage beasts," and when the Dominican raises the sacrament in the golden monstrance, they all fall to their knees.

When the Stranger next sees the monstrance, in the opening scene of Part III, it forces his gaze upward. Standing with the Dominican Confessor on the riverbank below the mountain, he watches a group of pilgrims gather for the Feast of Corpus Christi and hears them sing one of David's "Songs of Ascent":

> Blessed he who fears the Lord,
> who walks in his ways.

Who are these people, the Stranger asks. When he is told

they are people who have faith, he exclaims: "Then help me in my unbelief!" Then he sees the monstrance shining like a sun through the window of the monastery chapel.

But, as we might expect, there are countersigns. The main thrust of his spirit in Part II—the endeavor to understand his sufferings and to discern between the true and the illusory—persists. The main thrust of Part I—his looking outward, as a child does, at the delights and perils of the world around him—is also present, but less so. Gold, for instance, no longer has a hold over him, and he gives his silver watch to the ferryman ("I could never afford one of gold"). But the daughter of his first marriage is another matter—not so much Sylvia herself as his guilt in having failed her. When they meet on the riverbank, his moment of joy in her company is brief: The voice that used to remind him of the "willow warbler" reminds him now of the jay.

> But I am glad that we met once more, for there is nothing that binds me to earth any longer. (III,1)

Not even woman. Or so he says. But even as the setting sun makes a giant of his shadow and sends it climbing among the stars, the Lady appears behind him.

> Who is that disturbing my ascension?—trying to climb up over my shoulder? (III,1)

She is dressed in black: Mitzi, their little child, is dead.

> I am happy for the . . . child! For you I am sorry. I myself feel nothing. . . . (III,1)

He will not go down with her. Later, when she approaches him again, he says:

You—yet so unlike yourself! . . . You have grown so beautiful—as beautiful as you were when first I saw you—the day I asked you to let me be your friend, your slave. . . .

Now I can see your soul—the primary image, the angel, which—because of sin—was condemned to be imprisoned in the flesh. . . . There must be something higher, something beyond us, beyond the infinite past. . . . (III,2)

He remembers his dream: to find reconciliation, through woman, through *this* woman, purged now by suffering. Before his very eyes she changes into "a full-bosomed, motherly-looking woman with hair hanging loose." And he hears her say:

Come, my child, and I shall make amends for the wrong I once did you . . . upon my knee I shall cradle you to sleep. . . . Come—and let me heal your wounds—let me take the pain of your sufferings upon me! . . . Come! (III,3,ii)

He goes back down with her and for the first time calls her by her name, Ingeborg. Too soon she is Eve again. "I must have you at a distance," he says, "in order to be able to see you" (III,3,iv). Like Dante, "who possessed the soul of Beatrice throughout his life," but at a distance (III,3,ii).

THE STRANGER: If it is I who have made you evil, I beg you to forgive me, and I kiss your little hand—which could both caress me and scratch me—your little hand that guided me in the darkness—that led me on the long journey to Damascus. . . .

THE LADY: Does this mean good-by? *(Silence.)* It is your good-by, then? *(Silence. She leaves. . . .)* (III,3,iv)

But he is not left alone. The Tempter, whom he met once before at the crossroads, appears again.

His first appearance took place when the Stranger

found himself among the diseased "worshippers of Venus." They hail him as "Father." Why "Father"? Because they are the children of his teachings; by his teachings they were led into temptation. One of them claims to be his son Erik, and the Stranger, in horror, collapses in a faint. Nudging him with his foot, the Tempter says to the worshippers:

> You can make him believe anything you like! And that comes from his monstrous conceit and vanity! Has he not always acted as if the universe pivoted round him, as if he were the source and origin of all evil? The stupid fool has the fixed idea *he* was the one who taught youth to go in search of Venus! Ha! As if youth did not know about such things before he was born! His arrogance and conceit are insufferable, and he has been presumptuous enough to encroach upon and dabble in my profession. . . . Originally there were seven deadly sins—now there are eight. The eighth is my own invention. It is called despair.
>
> (III,2)

The temptation to despair is forged in a furnace of deceits. By unmasking the first deceit ("You are so far gone that you cannot tell your own children from others!"), the Tempter wins the Stranger's confidence, and makes the other deceits credible. Mouthing the Stranger's own thoughts, he turns them to his purposes ("Everything is revenged—even things we do thoughtlessly, imprudently. And who forgives us? The man who is generous and high-minded? Sometimes, yes! But divine justice—never!" [III,2]). Called in as a witness in a village trial ("of one of those strange birds who in their youth go in search of their Creator"), he erases everybody's guilt by going back over a series of seductions till he comes to Eve's seduction by the Serpent, then asks blasphemously: "Well, Serpent, who led *you* astray?" (III,3,i).

Once out of court, however, he speaks of women in

such terms that one might just as well say it was the woman who led the Serpent astray:

> They amount to nothing by themselves but mean everything to us, and are everything through us. They are our honor and our shame; our greatest joy, our deepest pain and distress; our redemption and our fall; our reward and our punishment; our strength and our weakness. (III,3,ii)

Poor women—they are nothing, and they are gods. Poor men, who can so deceive themselves. The Stranger, much deceived, returned to his Lady. Now, having left her again, he welcomes the company of the Tempter when the latter puts in a second appearance. "One ought never to talk about one's wife!" (III,3,iv). But they go on and on, until finally the Tempter covers his mouth: Perhaps he has said too much. When the Stranger's first wife appears on the scene and begs him to return to her, he turns away from her and once more starts up the mountain.

The monastery on the top of the mountain is, of course, unique. It is not to be identified with any existing Roman Catholic monastery; nevertheless, it is described in terms of that Church. The monk who leads the Stranger within its walls is a Dominican, a Roman Catholic priest. A statue of the Mother of Christ stands in the courtyard and in the middle of the chapter house there is an "enormously large crucifix." When the Stranger arrives, Mass is being celebrated. But confession is not needed here, because the monks "keep no secrets from one another." They are all "wise men whose lives have been out of the ordinary—each one unlike any of the others." Though they have "left the world," they are by no means cut off from it:

> The sciences and the fine arts are nourished here. . . . [There are] libraries and museums and laboratories, and an observatory. . . . Horticulture and agriculture are also studied and

carried on here; and a hospital for outsiders, with its own sulphur springs, is operated by the monastery. (III,4,i)

Dating from the time of Charlemagne, the monastery stands as "a monument to Western culture."

To be reconciled to mankind—that was the Stranger's "most secret desire" (III,3,ii). The monastery offers hope of its fulfillment. Here he meets the "werewolf," the Doctor whom he had wronged as a boy, now become Father Isidor. And Father Isidor forgives him: "With all my heart!" The Stranger had hoped to find reconciliation to mankind through the woman he married, precisely through her "womanness." He would speak of "mankind" as if woman were not really a part of it, or as if the reconciliation were only a matter of male getting along with female (III,3,ii). Does he begin to realize now that in Christ "there is neither male nor female" (Gal. 3:28), that men and women are persons first, and then male or female, and that reconciliation can only occur on the ground of personal being?

Perhaps. The question itself is caught up in the larger mystery of human existence. To probe that mystery further, he is led through a gallery of paintings by Father Melcher, a monk who has been through the trials not only "of this world of delusions" but "of misunderstanding, lies and contradictions as well." The gallery is filled with portraits of historical figures. They all have two heads: Boccaccio, in his youth a writer of godless stories, in his later days a saint; Luther, in his youth a champion of tolerance, in his later days of intolerance; Voltaire, the atheist who devoted his whole life to the defense of God. And so on, until the monk turns to the Stranger and concludes with a bit of Hegel, the philosopher who has "most successfully solved the contradictions of life and history and the spirit":

> Young man—well, you are relatively young—you started out in life by endorsing everything [thesis]; then you turned about and began to disavow and repudiate everything on principle [antithesis]. Now end your life by summarizing [synthesis]! In brief, be no longer one-sided! Do not say: either-or, but: both-and! In short: humanity and resignation! (III,4,ii)

To end his life by summarizing is, in effect, to begin anew. It is to be born again. "Now let us see if you can't become a child again," the Lady had said to him (I,1,i).

Only now does it make sense to look to "the 'Repetition' Kierkegaard talks about" for what it might have to say as to where the Stranger's journey has been leading. Repetition, for Kierkegaard, is essentially a religious movement effected by faith. When life has been fragmented by sin and the immediate relationship to God has been broken off, then "repetition is the restoration of the personality to its pristine integrity and the restoration of a new immediate God-relationship."[17] The Stranger's reconciliation to God should also mean reconciliation to himself and to mankind. To the extent that this is so, he is no longer a stranger to himself, no longer the unknown: his personality is restored. For him, then, repetition is the new birth, the answer to the question of Nicodemus: "How can a grown man be born again?" (John 3:4).

To ask the question and get an answer is not immediately to live that answer. The new birth implies a symbolic death—he shall lie in a coffin and then be "raised from the dead" and given a new name—but the Tempter will not let him die in peace. He summons up an image of a bride and bridegroom, "Adam and Eve in their paradise."[18]

> THE STRANGER: I, too, had my day in the sun once. . . . It was a day in spring—on a veranda—beneath the first tree to bear leaves—and a tiny coronet crowned her head—a white veil,

like a gentle mist, covered her countenance, which was not of this world. . . . And then came the darkness. . . .

THE TEMPTER: From where?

THE STRANGER: From the light itself! . . . That is all I know!

THE TEMPTER: It could not have been anything but a shadow; for without light there can be no shadow—but where there is darkness, there can be no light.

THE STRANGER: Stop! Or there will be no end to this! *(The Confessor and the Chapter enter in procession.)*

THE TEMPTER: *(as he disappears)* Farewell!

THE CONFESSOR: *(with a large black funeral pall)* May the Lord give him eternal rest!

THE CHOIR: And may perpetual light shine upon him!

THE CONFESSOR: *(covering the Stranger with the funeral pall)* May he rest in peace!

THE CHOIR: Amen! (III,4,iii)

In one sense the journey of the soul to God *(extra nos, intra nos, super nos)* is over; in another sense it has just begun.

For King Lear, at the moment of actual death, the possibility of faith is left open. For the Stranger, at the moment of his symbolic death, faith becomes a way of seeing in the darkness. Acting on that faith, he goes on hoping for true and lasting reconciliation, even though, as with Abraham, "it seemed his hope could not be fulfilled" (Rom. 4:18).

NOTES

1 *The Confession of a Fool (Le Plaidoyer d'un fou),* chap. 6.

2 Author's Note, *A Dream Play,* where he speaks of "his former dream play *Till Damaskus.*"

3 See Martin Lamm, *August Strindberg* (Stockholm, 1928); and for Part I, Evert Sprinchorn's footnotes to his translation in *The Genius of the Scandinavian Theater* (Mentor Books, 1964).

[4] See Raymond Williams, *Drama from Ibsen to Eliot* (Penguin Books, 1964, 1967), pp. 124ff. Gunnar Brandell makes these qualifications on the dream aspect of Part I: "What is pictured in *To Damascus* is not a dream or dreams. It is reality seen under a light that reminds one of that of dreams. Referring to Strindberg's own remarks, one finds that when he wrote the play he by no means conceived of it as a dream rendering. In a letter to his children he points out that the play is 'fantastic and spectacular' but also 'acted out in the present time and against a background of complete reality' (letter of May 24, 1898). In a letter to Geijerstam, Strindberg's formulation is even more precise: 'I would say it is a work of fiction with a terrifying half-reality behind it' (letter of March 17, 1898). ("Toward a New Art Form," in *The Genius of the Scandinavian Theater,* pp. 588–89).

[5] *Drama from Ibsen to Eliot,* p. 125.

[6] Charles Singleton, *An Essay on the Vita Nuova* (Cambridge, Mass.: Harvard University Press, 1949); Francis Fergusson, *Dante's Drama of the Mind.*

[7] *Dante's Drama of the Mind,* pp. 178–79.

[8] Throughout this chapter, the Part of the trilogy will be given in uppercase Roman numerals, the Act in Arabic numerals, and the Scene in lowercase Roman numerals. For Part I, I have used Evert Sprinchorn's translation, in *The Genius of the Scandinavian Theatre,* cited above; copyright 1964 by Evert Sprinchorn. Reprinted by permission. For Parts II and III, I have used Arvid Paulson's translation, in *Eight Expressionist Plays* (New York: Bantam Books, 1965); copyright 1963 by Arvid Paulson. Reprinted by permission.

[9] For a definition of "action," see chapter one, note 22.

[10] In certain places, we are told, "one can still discern the mythological memory of a lasting tension, and even a conflict," between men and women over the secret link that exists between spinning and sexuality. "The men and their gods, during the night, attack the spinsters, destroy their work, break their shuttles and weaving-tackle" (Mircea Eliade, *Myths, Dreams and Mysteries,* trans. by Philip Mairet [New York: Harper Torchbooks, 1967]).

[11] The Stranger comes dangerously close at times to making happiness itself the object of his search. And this is part of his problem, for happiness can never be an end in itself. "How well Kierkegaard expressed this in his maxim that the door to happiness opens outward. Anyone who tries to push this door open thereby causes it to close still more. The man who is desperately anxious to be happy thereby cuts off his own path to happiness. Thus in the

end all striving for happiness—for the supposed 'ultimate' in human life—proves to be in itself impossible" (Viktor E. Frankl, *The Doctor and the Soul* [New York: Bantam Books, 1967]).

[12] Quoted by Gunnar Brandell in the article already cited. Brandell comments: "Strindberg's idea of recurrence has nothing to do with Kierkegaard's Repetition, one of the Danish thinker's most obscure concepts. Repetition was for Kierkegaard the most difficult and most desirable condition of all, possible to attain only on the religious level, not on the esthetic or ethical level. For Strindberg the repetitions are partly a torture, partly a moral obligation. This twofold concept has a purely personal meaning and is most easily understood by recalling Strindberg's need to feel himself tested and castigated" (p. 595). Kierkegaard's Repetition does have something to do with the Stranger's journey, however, not at the end of Part I, but at the end of the trilogy.

[13] In *Jacob Wrestles,* which he broke off writing to begin *Damascus* I, Strindberg says: "The cross is for me the symbol of sufferings patiently borne and not as a token that Christ suffered in my stead; that is something I'm sure I must tend to myself. I have even framed a theory that goes like this: when we unbelievers refused to hear any more talk about Christ, He left us to our own devices, His vicarious satisfaction ceased, and we were left to get along as best we could with our miseries and our guilt feelings" (trans. by David Scanlan and Evert Sprinchorn, in *Inferno, Alone and Other Writings*). In the traditional Catholic view, the doctrine of Christ's vicarious sufferings never meant what Strindberg thought it meant. The doctrine is that the Son of God did indeed suffer and die for us, but this never meant that we would no longer have to suffer, no more than his death meant that we would no longer have to die. It is rather that his suffering and death, having found their meaning in the resurrection, give meaning to ours.

[14] "Kinuta," in *The Classic Noh Theatre of Japan,* by Ezra Pound and Ernest Fenollosa (New York: New Directions, 1959), p. 95.

[15] The alchemist has always worked within this spiritual horizon. Mircea Eliade writes: "The alchemist takes up and completes the work of Nature, working at the same time to 'perfect' himself. Gold is the noblest metal because it is perfectly 'mature'; if left in their chthonic womb, the other ores would turn into gold—but only after hundreds of thousands of centuries. Like the metallurgist, who transforms 'embryos' into metals by accelerating the growth begun within the Earth-Mother, so the alchemist dreams of intensifying that acceleration until the crowning and final transmutation of all the baser metals—'base' because still immature—into the

'noble' and perfectly 'ripe' metal, which is gold" (*Myths, Dreams and Mysteries,* p. 170).

[16] A Latin pun makes the Dominican a "Hound of the Lord" (*Domini-can*[*is*]).

[17] Reidar Thomte, *Kierkegaard's Philosophy of Religion,* p. 72. The young man in Kierkegaard's *Repetition* is deeply in love, but he realizes that marriage to his beloved would make them both unhappy. Still, he is engaged to the girl, and he is quite torn over what he should do. "Am I a victim of fate? Must I then be guilty and be a deceiver. . . ?" Then he learns that the girl has married someone else. He is free, and his freedom takes on for him a religious significance. "I am again myself," he cries. "This self which another would not pick up from the road I possess again. The discord in my nature is resolved, I am again unified. The terrors which found support and nourishment in my pride no longer enter in to distract and separate. Is there not a repetition? Did I not get everything doubly restored? Did I not get myself again, precisely in such a way that I must doubly feel its significance? And what is a repetition of earthly goods which are of no consequence to the spirit—what are they in comparison with such a repetition? Only his children Job did not receive again double, because a human life is not a thing that can be duplicated. In that case only spiritual repetition is possible, although in the temporal life it is never so perfect as in eternity, which is the true repetition" (*Repetition,* trans. with intro. and notes by Walter Lowrie [Princeton, N.J.: Princeton University Press, 1941], p. 144).

[18] C. E. W. L. Dahlstrom writes that "those critics motivated by certain religious prejudices will doubtless look upon this drama as a kind of high comedy." But an unprejudiced reading, he maintains, will prove otherwise. "Having lost hope of victory, he [the Stranger] yields to the negative forces; and thus the implications are tragic" ("Situation and Character in *Till Damaskus,*" *PMLA* LIII [1939]: 902). The fall of Adam and Eve can also be said to have tragic implications, but the loss of hope is not among them. To say that the Stranger has "lost hope of victory" is to be so "unprejudiced" as to blind oneself to the most basic movement of the religious spirit. That movement is a "passing-over" from death to life, whether that death be partial or definitive.

IV. THE COCKTAIL PARTY

I

The libation that brings the second act of *The Cocktail Party* to a close has produced in critics a variety of reactions, ranging from utter contempt to high praise, indicative, often enough, of their reaction to the play itself. To Rossell Hope Robbins the libation is "sheer nonsense," a "twentieth-century voodoo chant."[1] Wilbur Dwight Dunkel dismisses it as "a comical rite, not unlike the ornamentation of the grinning gargoyle on a medieval cathedral."[2] At the opposite pole, R. Gregor Smith considers it "the essence of the poet's pity and insight."[3] A more common reaction is to see it as what David E. Jones terms "rather like a solemn form of the toast to absent friends,"[4] or what W. K. Wimsatt, Jr., describes as "standing on choral and ritual tiptoe" but not entering the mysterious.[5]

There is no doubt that Eliot himself attached importance to the libation sequence. It recalls a similar sequence at the end of *The Family Reunion,* and it is the only sequence to which he has given ritual form; and thirdly, he has put it at the very end of the second act, a place of emphasis. The libation sequence has two parts: "The words for the building of the hearth," spoken for Edward and Lavinia Chamberlayne, whose marriage is remade in the course of the play, and "The words for those who go upon a journey," spoken for Celia Coplestone, who chooses to go the way of faith, "the kind of faith that issues from despair" (II,141).[6] The two sets of words close upon the past of each of the characters involved and open out upon the future. They point up the difference in quality, not so much of the choices made as of the characters making them. As we shall see, it is the difference between the wheel and the point.

In the first draft of the play, Eliot called these words "prayers."[7] They are, in fact, reminiscent of prayers in the Roman Ritual (used also in the Anglican). The Prayer for the Blessing of a House reads in part:

May it please you, O Lord,
to send down from heaven your holy angel.
May he watch over all who dwell in this house,
may he cherish and protect them always.

Here are Eliot's "words for the building of the hearth":

Let them build the hearth
Under the protection of the stars.
Let them place a chair each side of it.
May the holy ones ["winged ones," the first draft
reads] watch over the roof,
May the Moon herself influence the bed.
(II,149–50)

The *Itinerarium* reads in part:

O God, protect these pilgrims on their journey
as you protected Abraham in all his wanderings.
Be shade for them in the heat,
shelter in the rain,
a staff in insecurity,
a harbor in shipwreck.

Here are Eliot's "words for those who go upon a journey":

Protector of travellers
Bless the road.

Watch over her in the desert
Watch over her in the mountain
Watch over her in the labyrinth
Watch over her by the quicksand.
Protect her from the Voices
Protect her from the Visions
Protect her in the tumult
Protect her in the silence.

The three characters who speak these "prayers" are Julia, Alex and Reilly. They are clearly instruments of higher powers, the powers to whom they address their prayers. They address these powers as Protectors or Guardians, and the three of them, in turn, serve as guardians to whomever they judge to be in need of such service, moving from cocktail party to cocktail party. "It may be," says Celia, "that even Julia is a guardian. Perhaps she is *my* guardian" (I,2,69). Earlier in the same scene, the word *guardian* is used to refer to the innermost self, "the obstinate, the tougher self." In his first draft, Eliot spoke of this self as "the *daimon,* the genius"; it was E. Martin Browne, director of the play's première, who suggested the use of *guardian:*

Eliot accepted this suggestion because it did correspond to what he meant: influence of a spiritual kind may be exercised both within the self and by persons outside it.[8]

A Japanese critic has made the interesting observation that Alex and Julia function somewhat in the same way as the *waki,* or deuteragonist, in a Noh play, "urging on Reilly, the *shite* or protagonist, to formulate his judgment."[9] He does not develop the idea, however, and eventually discounts it. But in pursuing the matter further, I came to a better appreciation of the role of Alex, Julia and Reilly by regarding all three of them in the role of the *waki* in relation to Celia, and to Edward and Lavinia. The *waki* is a "Guest, or guests, very often a wandering priest."[10] In *Kayoi Kamachi,* for instance, the ghosts of the two lovers are brought together by the prayers of a priest. In embracing the teaching of Buddha, man and woman are able at last to embrace each other. *Nishikigi* tells a similar story: The two lovers are brought together in the dream of a pious priest. The ghost of the hero says:

> It is a good service you have done, sir,
> A service that spreads in two worlds,
> And binds up an ancient love
> That was stretched out between them.[11]

Assisted by Alex and Julia, Reilly performs a like service for Edward and Lavinia; he brings them "back from the dead" (I,3,71) in order to reunite them, the man who voiced his terror over "the death of the spirit" (II,113) and the woman "who had been only a ghost" to him (I,3,97). Like the *waki* in *Awoi No Uye,* Reilly also functions as exorcist, and not only Edward and Lavinia, but also Celia, perhaps especially Celia, are in need of this service. Referring to the choices open to her, he says:

> Both ways avoid the final desolation
> Of solitude in the phantasmal world
> Of imagination, shuffling memories and desires.
> CELIA: That is the hell I have been in.
>
> (II,142)

It is the fate of the exorcist, at one time or another, to be himself accused of being possessed, or in some way in league with the devil. Not even Jesus was spared that fate.[12] Reilly is three times called a devil by Celia (II,57, 58, 60), once by Edward, even if ambiguously (100), and once by Lavinia (117). But to each of them, when he has done his service, he is able to say: "Go in peace. And work out your salvation with diligence" (II,128,145). Viewing his role in terms of the *waki,* who, as we saw, is often a Buddhist priest, we can perhaps better appreciate what several critics have already pointed out: that these parting words are those of the dying Buddha to his disciples.

It is fitting, in view of his role, that Reilly should refer to himself, in a drinking song, as "the One Eyed Riley." The meaning of the one eye "is to be found, like so much else in *The Cocktail Party,* in a proverb: *In the kingdom of the blind the one-eyed man is king.*"[13] It is also to be found in a saying from the Sermon on the Mount:

> The light of the body is the eye:
> if therefore thine eye be single,
> the whole body shall be full of light.[14]

There is no doubt that Eliot attached some importance to the metaphor: The first draft of his play was entitled *One Eyed Riley.*[15] It is One Eyed Riley, together with his assistants, who leads the blind out of their private darkness. By removing the mote, as it were, from the eye, he will enable them to see what they must, to be single in intention, to choose the one way to which they are called. Edward and Lavinia choose to remake their marriage; Celia chooses to forgo marriage and to go the way whose "destination cannot be described." Which way is better?

> REILLY: Neither way is better.
> Both ways are necessary. It is also necessary
> To make a choice between them.
>
> (II,141)

It is time now to consider the choices made or, better, the characters who make them.

II

Celia is the most important character in the play. I state it baldly because it often goes unrecognized and is sometimes contradicted. Helen Gardner writes: "*The Cocktail Party* began as a play about marriage, and Edward and Lavinia are the central characters in its design."[16] It is true that Eliot began with Edward and Lavinia because his "point of departure" was the Alcestis myth, in which Alcestis, who dies for her husband Admetus, is given back to him by Heracles.[17] But what began as a play about a marriage ended as a play about something more. Nor is it correct to say that all his characters are created equal, as it were, though Eliot himself has been brought in support of this view. In an interview conducted for *The New York Times* in 1950, the interviewer states that "Eliot has said that he did not intend to portray one [character] as more important than the others."[18] We are not told where or when Eliot said this; the tense of the verb would seem to imply that he did *not* say it in the interview itself. In any case, in an interview published in the *Paris Review* nine years later, Eliot says quite the opposite:

> These two people [Edward and Lavinia] were the centre of the thing when I started and the other characters only developed out of it. The character of Celia, who came to be really the most important character in the play, was originally an appendage to a domestic situation.[19]

Possibly one reason why Celia is not always seen as the most important character in the play is that she does not appear in the third act (though her martyrdom is the main topic of conversation). It is the Chamberlaynes who carry the action of the third act. But that action is not the dramatic action of the play. The dramatic action of the play ended with the second act, when the two choices were made, the one by Edward and Lavinia, the other by Celia. "It is finished," says Reilly (II,145). Anything after that can only be by way of epilogue, or the beginning of another play. Eliot recognized that his third act was in the nature of an epilogue, but he thought that "the term 'epilogue,' read in the programme, is discouraging for the audience: it suggests that everything will be finished by then, and the epilogue may be omitted."[20]

I, for one, am more discouraged by the assumption that the natural rhythm of an action can be hidden merely by changing the label. If the feeling arises that the epilogue may be omitted, then perhaps it should be. But apparently Eliot never seriously considered omitting it. Nor did his director suggest it. After reading the first draft, E. Martin Browne felt that the playwright had left Celia's fate "as vague as, at the end of *The Family Reunion,* he had at first left Harry's."[21] Browne, of course, is not alone in requiring that the fates of the characters be more fully defined. Grover Smith, Jr., while expressing dissatisfaction with what Eliot does in the third act, feels that it "would be intolerable for the audience not to know whether Sir Henry's prescriptions worked; the curiosity, though diminished, is still alive."[22] But as far as the Chamberlaynes are concerned, why is it any more intolerable not to know how their "second marriage" turns out than not to know how the "second marriage" of Angelo and Mariana turns out in *Measure for Measure?* As for Peter Quilpe, at the end of the third act he has still not arrived at the point "where the words are valid." But Celia, like the Chamberlaynes, has arrived there by the end of the second act, and the point where the words are valid for the three of them is precisely the end point of the dramatic action.

Be that as it may, Browne's concern over Celia's fate stresses the importance he attached to her as the central character in the play. He knew that the presence of the Chamberlaynes in the last act, or epilogue, must not be allowed to overshadow her (though apparently, in the minds of many, it did just that): "She is the character whom above all we want to love—the heroine, the play's necessary focus of sympathy."[23]

III

To emphasize Celia's centrality is not to ignore the obvious importance of the Chamberlaynes (Edward more than Lavinia). The play opens with Edward's gradual disclosure that Lavinia has left him after five years of marriage. The rupture of one relationship brings to light the existence of several others. Edward, who is middle-aged, is in love with Celia, or thinks he is, and she with him. Lavinia also has turned to someone younger, a writer named Peter Quilpe, who, alas, has turned to Celia, though not she to him. If Edward and Lavinia are to find their way back to each other, it is through the maze of these relationships that they must come.

"What is hell?" Edward asks, and he answers, "Hell is oneself" (I,3,98). He has decided that he wants Lavinia back, but when, through Reilly's efforts, he has her back the next day, he finds himself more alone than ever. He experiences something of what Hopkins describes in one of his "Terrible Sonnets":

> Selfyeast of spirit a dull dough sours. I see
> The lost are like this, and their scourge to be
> As I am mine, their sweating selves; but worse.[24]

In this hell, all other figures are "merely projections" of oneself. When that self turns in upon itself, it finds it is empty, since it was never anything more than somebody else's projection. Edward sees that this is why he wanted his wife to come back; it was because of what she had made him into:

When I thought she had left me, I began to dissolve,
To cease to exist. That was what she had done to me!
I cannot live with her—that is now intolerable;
I cannot live without her, for she has made me incapable
Of having any existence of my own.
(II,112)

What Edward says is true, as far as it goes. And as Reilly tells him, Lavinia's situation is "much the same as your own" (II,115). But what Reilly has to make both of them see is that they are "the self-deceivers / Taking infinite pains, exhausting their energy, / Yet never quite successful" (II,119). Both of them had lied to him about their respective lovers, and behind that lie was the lie they had been telling the self about the self. For Edward, the lie that he has yet to admit began to surface with the discovery that he was never really in love with Celia Coplestone; for Lavinia, with the discovery that Peter Quilpe had never really been in love with her. To Edward, Reilly says:

You liked to think of yourself as a passionate lover.
Then you realised, what your wife has justly remarked,
That you had never been in love with anybody;
Which made you suspect that you were incapable
Of loving.
(II,123)

To Lavinia:

You had wanted to be loved;
You had come to see that no one had ever loved you.
Then you began to fear that no one *could* love you.
(II,124)

To both:

> And now you begin to see, I hope,
> How much you have in common. The same isolation.
> A man who finds himself incapable of loving
> And a woman who finds that no man can love her.
>
> (II,125)

What are they to do? Edward had hoped to be sent to Reilly's sanatorium in order to escape Lavinia. Lavinia thought she had already been there, and been changed by the experience. But Reilly tells her that she has never visited *his* sanatorium; the people he sends there are not easily deceived. Neither Edward nor Lavinia is fit for his sanatorium: It would be a horror beyond their imagining, they would become "prey / To the devils who arrive at their plenitude of power / When they have you to themselves." What can they do when they can go neither backward nor forward? They must make the best of a bad job.

> REILLY: When you find, Mr. Chamberlayne,
> The best of a bad job is all any of us make of it—
> Except of course, the saints—such as those who go
> To the sanatorium—you will forget this phrase,
> And in forgetting it will alter the condition.
>
> (II,126)

Together they leave to "work out their salvation with diligence," and to set themselves once more "to the building of the hearth." When Celia enters Reilly's office, we know that we shall hear more about the "saints" and the "sanatorium" to which they go.

IV

Celia's first reaction to Edward's news that Lavinia has left him is in terms of her own affair with him. "Doesn't that settle all our difficulties?" When she discovers that Reilly has "bewitched" him into wanting Lavinia back, she refuses to believe that he is sincere: He must have surrendered to fatigue, or panic or vanity. But eventually she comes to see that the man she is speaking to is not the man she loved:

> I see you as a person whom I never saw before.
> The man I saw before, he was only a projection—
> I see that now—of something that I wanted—
> No, not *wanted*—something I aspired to—
> Something that I desperately wanted to exist.
> It must happen somewhere—but what, and where is it?
> (I,2,67)

Celia will go on searching. In his essay on Baudelaire, Eliot provides a kind of map for this journey of the spirit:

> The romantic idea of Love [in Baudelaire] is never quite exorcised, but never quite surrendered to. In *Le Balcon, . . .* one of Baudelaire's most beautiful poems, there is all the romantic idea, but something more: the reaching out towards something which cannot be had *in,* but which may be had partly *through,* personal relations. Indeed, in much romantic poetry the sadness is due to the exploitation of the fact that no human relations are adequate to human desires, but also to the disbelief in any further object for human desires than that which, being human, fails to satisfy them.[25]

Celia, however, believes that there *is* some further object, something that she not merely wants, but aspires to. She had reached out for it in her relations with Edward and been disappointed. It was not to be found *in* those relations, but it may be had partly *through* them. Those relations had quickened her desire for it and at the same time brought her to the realization that she must search beyond them. The Stranger in *Till Damaskus* would have understood her.

What she describes to Reilly as her "awareness of solitude" stems from this realization:

> . . . it isn't that I *want* to be alone,
> But that everyone's alone—or so it seems to me.
> They make noises, and think they are talking to each
> other;
> They make faces, and think they understand each
> other.
>
> (II,134)

Celia speaks out of her own anguish, and she is blunt, even cruel. But she is aware that to continue on her way, in search of that "further object," will not make her any less alone. Reilly confirms this: Her way, like the way she is renouncing, "means loneliness—and communion." Those who take the other way "Can forget their loneliness. You will not forget yours" (II,142).

There is still another feeling, rising from the very ground of her being, that comes with the realization that she must go on searching. She suffers, she says, from "a sense of sin."

> It's not the feeling of anything I've ever *done,*
> Which I might get away from, or of anything in me
> I could get rid of—but of emptiness, of failure
> Towards someone, or something, outside of myself;
> And I feel I must . . . *atone*—is that the word?
>
> (II,136–37)

This disclosure is crucial to an understanding of the spirit that urges Celia on. Her feeling is one that is very difficult to convey, and for those who have never experienced it very difficult to grasp. The attempt to convey it is the greatest challenge that Eliot has presented to the actress in the role of Celia. The feeling that Celia is trying to express is exactly that which Rudolf Otto describes in his famous work *The Idea of the Holy:*

> The feeling is beyond question not that of the transgression of the moral law, however evident it may be that such a transgression, where it has occurred, will involve it as a consequence: it is the feeling of absolute "profaneness." . . . He, only, who is "in the Spirit" knows and feels what this "profaneness" is; but to such an one it comes with piercing acuteness, and is accompanied by the most uncompromising judgement of self-depreciation, a judgement passed, not upon his character, because of individual "profane" actions of his, but upon his own very existence as creature before that which is supreme above all creatures. And at the same time he passes upon [that which is supreme] a judgement of *appreciation* of a unique kind by the category diametrically contrary to "the profane," the category "holy" . . . [p.51].
> [Atonement] amounts to a longing to transcend this sundering unworthiness, given with the self's existence as "creature" and profane natural being [p.55].[26]

Celia's sense of sin—"not the feeling of anything I've ever *done*"—is nothing other than Otto's "feeling of absolute 'profaneness.' " Her feeling of "emptiness, of failure," is his "uncompromising judgement of self-depreciation" before that which is supreme above all creatures, before "someone, or something," as she says, "outside of myself." Issuing from that feeling of "failure" is her desire to atone —to become "at-one" with that someone outside the self, who is not profane, but holy. Perfect atonement must mean the total giving of one's self, losing oneself in order to find it.

Her condition, Reilly tells her, is "curable." But the form of treatment must be her own choice. If she wishes, he can reconcile her to the human condition, "the condition to which some who have gone as far as you / Have succeeded in returning." They may remember the vision that they had, but they do not repine,

Are contented with the morning that separates
And with the evening that brings together
For casual talk before the fire
Two people who know they do not understand each other,
Breeding children whom they do not understand
And who will never understand them.

(II,140)

But Celia feels that to give up her vision would be "a kind of surrender—No, not a surrender—more like a betrayal." She doesn't want to forget it, she wants to live with it. She "could do without everything, / Put up with anything," if she might cherish it. She feels it would be dishonest for her, now, "to try to make a life with *any*body!" She couldn't give anyone "the kind of love" which belongs to that life. And if there is no other way, ". . . then I feel just hopeless." Reilly understands: There *is* another way, he tells her, but it requires faith, precisely that kind of faith "that issues from despair":

The destination cannot be described;
You will know very little until you get there;
You will journey blind. But the way leads towards possession
Of what you have sought for in the wrong place.

(II,141)

It is at this point that Reilly tells her neither way is better, both ways are necessary, and a choice must be made between them. Celia chooses the second way, "not frightened but glad" to be told that it is "a terrifying journey" (II, 142).[27]

V

Celia, it is true, does not question Reilly's assumption that to marry is to turn one's vision into memory.

What she says, in effect, is that *for her* marriage is out of the question. She chooses rather to go to Reilly's sanatorium. What is that sanatorium? It is not "a kind of hotel." That was where Lavinia went. Not very many go to his sanatorium. Nothing is forced on them. Some of them return, "in a physical sense." But no one disappears, and some lead very active lives in the world. The sanatorium, then, is the place where one goes to pursue one's religious vision. If one must define it further, it is a retreat house where spiritual exercises are given, aimed precisely at helping the retreatant choose his state in life or specify a choice already made. Since he need not return "in a physical sense," we must suppose that this retreat house is also a convent or monastery, as is sometimes the case. Celia chooses to join a nursing order of nuns and to serve the natives of Kinkanja, by whom she is martyred. But in terms of dramatic action, the crucial choice has already been made: She has chosen to follow her religious vision.

The dramatic action sets up a contrast not so much between two ways of life as between characters, pointing up a diversity that exists among all God's creatures. "The sun has its brightness, the moon a different brightness, and the stars a different brightness, and the stars differ from each other in brightness" (1 Cor. 15:41). There are, as John McLaughlin puts it, "degrees of perfection which vary according to the spiritual capacity of the individual."[28] To see the contrast in terms of character is at least consistent with Eliot's view, given in connection with *The Cocktail Party,* that "we should turn away from the Theatre of Ideas to the Theatre of Character."[29]

It is, however, impossible to talk about Eliot's characters without talking about his ideas. In the first draft of the play, he has Reilly say of the Chamberlaynes, after their interview with him: "They accept the wheel."[30] In the final version, the line reads: "They accept their destiny" (II,149). The meaning remains unchanged, but the image of the wheel, unclear in the context because too isolated, borrows light from other uses that Eliot has made of it.

In the opening Chorus of *The Rock,* the wheel appears as the "perpetual revolution of configured stars," the "world of spring and autumn, birth and dying." It is the "endless cycle of idea and action, / Endless invention, endless experiment," which "Brings knowledge of motion, but not of stillness." Stillness lies at the center of the wheel, at the heart of reality, for there God's will, itself unmoved, moves all, "the still point of the turning world" *(Coriolan* and *Burnt Norton).* Like Dante, Eliot believes that God's will is our peace. Only the fool, says Becket in *Murder in the Cathedral,* thinks he "can turn the wheel on which he turns." This is another way of saying that sin is the attempt to break out of time, to force God's will.[31] To "accept the wheel" is to "accept one's destiny." And for the Chamberlaynes, as for most of us, that means making "the best of a bad job."

"Except of course, the saints." Within the perpetual revolution of configured stars there will be degrees of brightness, but for those stars that glow at the still point, a leap in brightness. These are the saints. This is Celia. Not only does she accept the wheel, but by entering the stillness of the dynamic point, she helps radiate its peace and power.

> Men's curiosity searches past and future
> And clings to that dimension. But to apprehend
> The point of intersection of the timeless
> With time, is an occupation for the saint—
> No occupation either, but something given
> And taken, in a lifetime's death in love,
> Ardour and selflessness and self-surrender.
>
> *(The Dry Salvages,* V)

Time is to the timeless as the rim of the wheel is to its center. If the timeless is to intersect with time, we must imagine the power and peace of the still point radiating like spokes to the rim, imparting both motion and harmony. Jesus' redemptive death was the major historical moment of such an intersection, so special in its implications that it gave meaning to all other intersections:

> A moment in time but time was made through that moment:
> for without the meaning there is no time, and that
> moment of time gave the meaning.
>
> (*The Rock,* VII)[32]

In the third act of the play, Eliot tries to bring Celia's death into this series of intersections of the timeless with time. "She paid the highest price / In suffering," Reilly says. "That is part of the design" (182). And apparently Edward's reaction is also part of the design:

> But if this was right—if this was right for Celia—
> There must be something else that is terribly wrong,
> And the rest of us are somehow involved in the wrong.
>
> (183)

It is the same view that Eliot expresses in one of his notes to *The Idea of a Christian Society:* "The notion of communal responsibility, of the responsibility of every individual for the sins of the society to which he belongs, is one that needs to be more firmly apprehended."[33]

Though we may quarrel with Eliot's dramatic presentation of this idea in the third act, we can acknowledge the drama of the two acts leading up to it—the drama of three people's journey (four, if we count Peter), in and through personal relationships, in search of human fulfillment. The dramatic focus favors Celia's journey. When we leave the Stranger at the end of *Till Damaskus,* faith has become for him a way of knowing. For Celia, it is more than that. It is also a way of loving.

NOTES

[1] *The T. S. Eliot Myth* (New York: Henry Schuman, 1951), pp. 42, 92.

[2] "T. S. Eliot's Quest for Certitude," *Theology Today* VII, No. 2 (July, 1950): 234.

[3] "An Exchange of Notes on T. S. Eliot," *Theology Today* VII, No. 4 (January, 1951): 505.

[4] *The Plays of T. S. Eliot* (London: Routledge & Kegan Paul, 1960), p. 124.

[5] "Eliot's Comedy," *Sewanee Review* LVIII (Autumn, 1950): 675.

[6] Page references are to the 1950 edition of *The Cocktail Party* (New York: A Harvest Book, Harcourt, Brace & World). Copyright 1950 by T. S. Eliot. Reprinted by permission of Harcourt Brace Jovanovich, Inc.

[7] E. Martin Browne, *The Making of a Play* (Cambridge: University Press, 1966), p. 18.

[8] Browne, p. 15.

[9] Tsuneari Fukada, "God Present though Absent: Reflections on *The Cocktail Party*," in *T. S. Eliot: A Tribute from Japan*, eds. Masao Hirai and E. W. F. Tomlin (Tokyo: The Kenyusha Press, 1966), p. 173.

[10] Ezra Pound and Ernest Fenollosa, *The Classic Noh Theatre of Japan* (New York: New Directions, 1959), p. 15.

[11] Pound and Fenollosa, p. 82.

[12] Matt. 12:24; John 8:48, 10:21. Herbert Knust observes how the god Wotan's power "appeared devilish to the uninitiated," but proved benevolent to those who trusted him ("What's the Matter with One-Eyed Riley?," *Comparative Literature* XVII, No. 4: 293.

[13] William Arrowsmith, "English Verse Drama II: *The Cocktail Party*," *The Hudson Review* III, No. 3 (Autumn, 1950): 413.

[14] Matt. 6:22. This is the King James version. The Douay also reads "if therefore thine eye be *single*." Even though most modern versions translate the Greek απλους, more accurately, as *sound* or

healthy, the saying has come into the language as having reference to singleness of intention.

[15] Browne, p. 26.

[16] "The Comedies of T. S. Eliot," in *T. S. Eliot: The Man and His Work,* ed. Allen Tate (New York: Delacorte Press, 1966), p. 164. Also Jones, p. 124; Eric Bentley, *The Dramatic Event* (New York: Horizon Press, 1954), p. 233; Philip R. Headings, *T. S. Eliot* (New York: Twayne Publishers, 1964), p. 149.

[17] For discussion of Eliot's use of the myth see: Robert B. Heilman, "*Alcestis* and *The Cocktail Party,*" *Comparative Literature* V (Spring, 1955): 105–16, and William Arrowsmith, "The Comedy of T. S. Eliot," in *English Stage Comedy,* ed. W. K. Wimsatt, Jr. (New York: Columbia University Press, 1955), pp. 148–72.

[18] Foster Hailey, "An Interview with T. S. Eliot," *The New York Times,* April 16, 1950, Section 2, p. 1.

[19] Donald Hall, "T. S. Eliot: The Art of Poetry I" (Interview), *Paris Review* XXI (Spring-Summer, 1959): 61.

[20] Browne, p. 9.

[21] Browne, p. 22.

[22] *T. S. Eliot's Poetry and Plays* (Chicago: University of Chicago Press, 1950 and 1956), p. 216.

[23] Browne, p. 40. Since the writing of this chapter, E. Martin Browne has published an expanded version of "The Making of a Play" as a chapter in his book *The Making of T. S. Eliot's Plays* (New York: Cambridge University Press, 1969). Because he directed the first productions of all of Eliot's plays beginning with *The Rock,* his book is a unique document, and a thing of joy.

[24] *Poems and Prose of Gerard Manley Hopkins,* selected with an introduction and notes by W. H. Gardner (Baltimore: Penguin Books, 1956), No. 44, p. 62. In *The Making of T. S. Eliot's Plays,* Browne writes: "I remember vividly one incident at the dress rehearsal. I was sitting in the front row of the dress-circle, and Eliot was immediately behind me. As Edward spoke the line

Hell is oneself

near the end of his quarrel with Lavinia, Eliot leaned over and whispered: 'Contre Sartre.' The line, and the whole story of Edward and Lavinia, are his reply to 'Hell is other people' in *Huis Clos*" (p. 233).

[25] *Selected Essays* (New York: Harcourt, Brace & Co., 1932), p. 343.

[26] *The Idea of the Holy* (New York & London: Oxford University Press, 1958; first published in 1923).

[27] Reilly *says* that neither way is better, but in the passage quoted above about the people who have given up their vision, he manages to convey quite the opposite impression. Eliot has cautioned those people "who want to get a general statement on marriage out of the relations of Edward and Lavinia. You can't depict all of your views about life. You are limited by time" (*New York Times* interview). But the problem is with the general statement that Eliot puts on the lips of *Reilly*. It is one thing to say that two people short on vision can marry and be merry, and another thing to say that to marry is to turn one's vision into memory. Considered in relation to Celia, Reilly's statement is "true in the metaphysical order without further qualifications. The mediocre spirit because of its limited capacity can never 'understand' (act) to the extent of the heroic soul" (John J. McLaughlin, S.J., "A Daring Metaphysic: *The Cocktail Party*," *Renascence* III, No. 1 [Autumn, 1950]: 22). But Reilly isn't talking about mediocre spirits; he is talking about spirits who "have gone as far" as Celia. Must we assume, then, that marriage inevitably makes such spirits mediocre? Historically, marriage in the Western world has suffered in relation to passion, on the one hand, and to celibacy, on the other. Denis de Rougemont's *Love in the Western World* (New York: Fawcett World Library, 1966) is all about the former, and John T. Noonan's *Contraception* (New York: A Mentor-Omega Book, 1967), which is nothing less than a history of human sexuality, deals in more than one section with the latter.

[28] "A Daring Metaphysic: *The Cocktail Party*," p. 16.

[29] Answer to Question 12, *World Review*, November, 1949, as quoted in Raymond Williams, *Drama from Ibsen to Eliot*, p. 267.

[30] Browne, p. 17.

[31] See Chapter I.

[32] It is not easy to pin down Eliot's concept of time. The wheel, as an image of cyclic time, is not to be identified with it; he uses the image rather to show time's relation to eternity. The future, for him, is not a mere repetition of the past: "Fare forward, travellers! . . . You are not the same people who left that station . . ." *(The Dry Salvages)*. But, as William F. Lynch, S.J., describes it, "he seems to place our faith, our hope, and our love, not in the flux of time but in the *points* of time. I am sure his mind is interested in the line and time of Christ, whose Spirit is his total flux. But I am not sure about his imagination. Is it or it is not an imagination saved from time's nausea or terror by points of intersec-

tion?" (*Christ and Apollo,* New York: Sheed & Ward, 1960; A Mentor-Omega Book, 1963 [p. 171]). As far as *The Cocktail Party* is concerned, I submit that his imagination tries to keep the horizontal and the vertical aspects of time in tension. Celia journeys "blind" in the sense that her "destination cannot be described," and she accepts the fact that her journey through time will be "terrifying," but what gives her the courage to make the journey is her "vertical" apprehension of the still point. Faring forward, she apprehends more deeply, in the hope of full possession. See Nikolai Berdyaev's *Slavery and Freedom* (New York: Charles Scribner's Sons, 1944), for what he calls existential time, "best symbolized not by the circle nor by the line but by the point" (p. 260).

[33] Quoted by Louis L. Martz in connection with *Murder in the Cathedral.* "The Wheel and the Point," *Sewanee Review,* Winter, 1947: 126–47; also in *T. S. Eliot: A Selected Critique,* ed. Leonard Unger (New York: Rinehart & Co., 1948), pp. 444–62.

V. BREAK OF NOON

I

A blazing sun cuts through the flesh of this play like a two-edged sword. It is the sun of high noon, dividing the morning that was "so beautiful" from the evening that will be "still more beautiful." It is the noonday sun at the center of our lives: "Behind us is that huge past pushing with an irresistible force, and ahead of us the huge future which inhales us with an irresistible force." It is the consuming sun of a woman's love, a sun which "rises naked" and tears the self away from itself. It is the incandescent sun of God's love, dividing man from woman only to reunite them in a midnight pierced by a million stars: "All those stars in the sky," the woman says. "They hit me square in the face, like a sunstroke."

Under this blazing sun, on the deck of a boat in the middle of the Indian Ocean, turned now into a "desert of fire," Claudel brings together his four characters—Ysé, the woman; Mesa, the man; De Ciz, the husband; Amalric, the lover. They are all on a journey to China, all (to use Dante's phrase) in the middle of the journey of their lives. When the eight bells sound at noon, at the end of Act One, a change will have taken place in all their lives. Deep inside them it is waiting to erupt into action. This is the "divide," the *partage* of the French title: *Partage de Midi.*[1]

The most crucial change, in terms of dramatic interest, is the change in the life of Mesa. He moves from the desert of self-love to the closed-in bay of a woman's love and from there, with woman still at his side, to the open sea of the love or God.

II

In a program note for Jean-Louis Barrault's successful production of the play at the Théâtre Marigny, on December 17, 1948, forty-three years after the play was written, Claudel describes Mesa in terms of the "huge past" pushing against him: He is a man who has received, "in spite of himself, the call of God, a call that cannot be denied." After a long resistance, he decided to answer it. But when he presented himself at the altar, God said *no*, "a peremptory *no* without any explanation." Mesa turned away, but that inexorable call went with him. What is it God wants? Now he is on his way to an important position in China, an exile in the middle of the ocean, and now it is noon.[2]

Ysé, at one point, cruelly refers to Mesa as a "sacre petit bourgeois," and Claudel, looking back over his own youth, heartily concurs, calling him among other things "un avare, un egoïste."[3] "I don't worry about other people," Mesa says to Ysé, and when she chides him, he retorts: "But it's true. Does this mean that I think only of myself?" Ysé laughs and says:

> Are you discovering this for the first time? Try to deny that women are useful. It's a comfortable feeling just to be concerned with oneself. One never tires of looking at oneself, because one is so infinitely nice. I know people who are always ready to offer themselves, but to give oneself for good is something quite different. (I,42–43)

And so he must face the desert of self-love within him, as difficult to look upon as "this desert of a sea" on which he sails. And he must face Ysé. "Forty days on that boat," he will say later. "And for forty days there I was facing her" (III,108). It is his place of temptation, prowled by the noonday devil.[4]

What does it mean to love? He wants to know. All the same, he ventures to say that he understands. Ysé ridicules the idea: "You don't need to understand, dear sir, you need to lose consciousness." If *she* cannot, it is because she is "too wicked." But to love—it's like ether.

You remember about the sleep of Adam. It's in the catechism. That's the way they made the first woman. A woman, Mesa, just give it a moment's thought. One inside the other, all the beings there are to infinity inside that one creature. You might as well acknowledge it. She has to die in the arms of the man who loves her. (I,25)

What does one ask of woman? He imagines that to ask the question seriously would provoke in him "a terrible upheaval, a terrible disturbance of one's substance." And yet "everything in him demands everything in a woman." The very thought seems to fill him with anger. "What is there between you and me?" Six bells sound. It is one hour till noon.

YSÉ: Mesa, I am Ysé.
MESA: It's too late. Everything is over. Why did you come to talk with me again?
YSÉ: Because I found you.
MESA: I tell you that everything is over! I wasn't expecting you. I had made careful plans to retire, to withdraw from mankind, yes, from all of mankind. Why not? I had actually accomplished it. Why did you come to talk with me again? Why did you come to upset me?
YSÉ: Women are created just for that reason. (I,30–31)

In *Le Soulier de satin* Claudel expounds in a much more didactic fashion this "reason" for woman's existence. Dona Prouheze is told by her Guardian Angel that she was intended not only as a "catch" for Rodrigo but also as a "bait." There was no other way to get him to understand his neighbor, to get inside his skin; to get him to understand the dependence of another on him. But "man in woman's arms," the woman says, "forgets God." Not so. In woman's arms man is bound up in the mystery of God's creation; he crosses again for a moment into Eden. "Love without the sacrament, is it not sin?" Yes, but "sin also serves," says the Angel, voicing the epigraph to the play: St. Augustine's *Etiam peccata.*[5]

Claudel's idea that woman is a "bait" God uses to involve a man with mankind is very much like Strindberg's dream of man's reconciliation to mankind through woman. But there is a difference. With Claudel, woman succeeds in her vocation. Furthermore, in both *Partage* and *Soulier,* Claudel goes beyond his own didacticism. If woman brings man to reconciliation in God, man brings woman—a movement of no dramatic import in *Road to Damascus.*

"Do you believe in God?" Mesa asks Ysé. "I don't know," she answers. "I never thought of it." She will have occasion to think of it later. As for Mesa, he is filled with God and has had enough:

> . . . imagine someone within you—and this sounds ridiculous—forever! Another person in you and whom you have to tolerate. He lives and I live. He thinks and I weigh His thought in my heart. It was He who made my eyes. Couldn't I at least see Him? It was He who made my heart and I can't get rid of Him. You don't understand. But it is not a question of understanding. I am speaking about eyes which just in looking at you make you comprehensible. The torment of feeling oneself studied, spelled out by someone who never comes to the end of what He is doing. (I,33)

Ysé may not understand him, but what she does understand is that he is unhappy.

MESA: At least that belongs to me.
YSÉ: Yes, that is so. Wouldn't it be better if I belonged to you? (I,35)

But that is impossible. Why is it only now that he has met her? She is married and her husband and child are with her; worse still, Amalric, her former lover, is after her again. But it is hard not to be loved. "I was made for happiness! . . . It is hard to wait!"

And here I am at this time of noon when I see so clearly what is very near, so near that I can see nothing else. And behold! you are here! How close the present seems! What is immediate is close at hand like something having the force of necessity! My strength has gone. Oh God! I . . . I cannot wait any longer! (I,37)

Ysé is suddenly afraid. Mesa must not love her. She bids him say after her that he will not love her. In saying it over and over again, he pours out his love for her: "Ysé, I will not love you." Noon is about to sound. Eight bells. The time of temptation has passed. In his heart, which can wait no longer, Mesa has already broken out of time: Now he has but to find the place.

III

From the desert of self-love Mesa moves to the closed-in bay of a woman's love. Standing behind her in a Hong Kong cemetery, his hands without actually touching her go over all her body. Little by little, with increasing fervor, they take possession of her.

MESA: Oh Ysé! What I am doing is forbidden.
YSÉ: Are you sure? I didn't know that I was forbidden.
MESA: I am thinking of the boat which brought us, and its own smoke that it disappeared into when we watched it leave.
YSÉ: It is not a boat you are holding in your arms, but a living woman.
MESA: Oh Ysé, don't let me come back!
YSÉ: I am yielding to you. I am yours.
MESA: She said: I yield. I am yours.
YSÉ: And you have to yield to me.
MESA: I am holding it, ready to leave on it. I am holding my huge boat.[6] (II,67)

Mesa and Ysé are standing in the center of an empty Chinese tomb, a hemicycle in the form of an Omega surrounded by bamboo: "This kind of Omega is like arms coming to get you and then holding you warmly. In the open air. There is no way of escaping if you want to." That is Mesa's feeling when he first arrives there to wait for Ysé. He knows he is caught. His soul has given out. "All is finished." The mast of the boat to which he is bound has become a cross—"a great cross," Ysé will say of herself (III,118). But the cross is an instrument of transfiguration.

Before going to Mesa, Ysé takes definitive leave of her husband, De Ciz. He is about to go on a business trip, in rather questionable circumstances. Ysé pleads with him not to be away from her "in the middle of her life." Ten years she gave him. "To think that now I'm thirty, and my youth is over, and what I could give you is over. I've given it all." Not quite all:

If any man had me, I would want to keep him from having anything else. If I am his, isn't that enough? I haven't given you the complete self that I am. There is a certain death that I can give. But I knew that you were not serious. Fundamentally not serious. (II,61)

Mesa is serious. Recognizing this, Ysé says of her husband: "If he dies, it will be a good thing." Mesa, as Jacques Madaule observes, is made to play David to his Uriah:[7] Send him into the thick of danger and let him die. As Customs Commissioner, with important connections, Mesa offers him a good job, but reminds him that the country is seething with revolution and that the danger from pirates, fever and poisoning is not to be discounted. "I wouldn't hesitate myself, but I am not married." His wife has nothing to do with it, De Ciz says. "Mesa, I'm your man." A knife is a narrow blade but the two halves of the fruit it cuts will never be rejoined. So said Ysé. And to Mesa:

. . . There is no past now, and no future, no husband, no children, nothing, nothing, *nada!* nothing at all! You want to know the reason? I am the reason. Now tell me if that isn't what you expected.
MESA: You are the reason.
YSÉ: I am the reason. I am Ysé, your soul. (II,73)

Mesa was a man of desire, desperately yearning in the depths of his being for happiness. Is it possible that Ysé is happiness? "No. You are what is in the place of happiness." She is the sun, and she is not the sun. Once, while still on the boat, Mesa, pointing to the sun, had said: "There is our home, fellow wanderers!" And Ysé had said: "He is too strong for me! I wish night would come! I am like an animal that lives only at night" (I,11). Now, all through the scene, an eclipse of the sun is about to take place, with gongs and firecrackers sounding intermittently: "The sun mustn't be devoured that easily by an evil dragon." At one point, Mesa frees himself abruptly from Ysé's arms.

YSÉ: What is it?
MESA: Nothing. I thought someone was calling me. (II,74)

IV

When the last act of the play opens, Ysé has left Mesa and is living with Amalric. Or rather, she is facing death with him. Caught in the Boxer Uprising, they have taken refuge in the ruins of a Confucian temple. Amalric will make sure that they are not taken alive; he will set a time bomb, and they will disappear "in a clap of thunder."

Gabriel Marcel, who considers *Partage de Midi,* in substance, one of the richest of plays, feels nevertheless that it was dramatically wrong to have placed between acts a crisis so serious that it could take Ysé from Mesa's arms and propel her into the arms of Amalric.[8] Has Mesa renounced his love for Ysé? Or has Ysé simply left him? There is something to be said for Marcel's objection, especially when one considers how important a place Claudel gives to renunciation in the achieving of human fulfillment. "Sacrifice," he writes, "somehow provokes the Divine part. By willingly withdrawing, we make room for an incited action of Grace, as it were; we are playing on the side of the All Powerful for an enormous profit."[9] This idea is nothing more or less than the Christian paradox: "The man who loses himself for my sake will find himself. What does it profit a man if he wins the whole world and loses his very self?" (Luke 9:24–25). Mesa, before giving his soul to Ysé and taking hers, "like quick lime compelling the sand as it burns and hisses," was well aware of the wager implicit in his decision: "Inside, my soul is like a gold piece in the fingers of a gambler. Heads or tails. No, not gold. Lead" (II,56). Has he taken his soul in his own hands again? Did he ever really give it? Or has Ysé scorned the gift?

Ysé had wished for the night to come, but the night is their undoing. In his poem *Ténèbres,* written in 1905, the same year that *Partage* was begun, Claudel sees the night as a symbol of separation:

> I am here, the other is elsewhere, and the silence
> is complete:
> We are the most wretched of beings, and Satan sifts
> us like wheat.
>
> I suffer, the other suffers, and there is no strand
> On which to meet, from her to me no word, no hand,
> Nothing in common between us but the night incom-
> municable,
> The night that makes an end of work and the fearful
> love, the love impracticable.[10]

With Mesa and Ysé, darkness has had its way. In the course of Act Three we learn that Mesa had indeed begun in his heart to pull away from Ysé, and Ysé, sensing this, left him, carrying his child in her womb.

To Amalric she says:

> With all of his being, but secretly and slyly, he wanted me to leave. Did he think I couldn't read that in his eyes? It is true that I had to leave. I asked him if he was happy, and he looked at me with that expression on his face of a bad priest. (III,96)

Amalric doubts that Mesa really loved her. "He loved me," she protests, "as you will never love me. And I loved as I will never love you." It is duty, not love, that joins her to Amalric:

> You enslaved me, but you don't know what a woman is who is not enslaved. You don't know the desert of a woman, and the thirst, and the pain of love, and the knowledge that the other is alive, and the moment when each looks into the eyes of the other. You don't know what it is when another soul is thrust into yours. One whole year! It lasted one whole year. I felt he

was a captive but I did not own him and there was something foreign and impossible in him. (III,96)

And so she came to Amalric, and when the child was born, he loved it, "as if I had made it." But now the sun is going down and soon they must dic.

YSÉ: It is terrible to be dead. Amalric, tell me the the truth. Are you sure that there is no God?
AMALRIC: Why should there be? If there was one, I would have told you. (III,93–94)

But he and she do exist, they are creatures of reality. "No dreams, just realities." Like that sun which during all this time has finished with the business of setting. "Can a man live without the sun?" Amalric goes off to make the rounds, and Mesa appears out of the darkness.

His soul overflows in a torrent of words, but Ysé remains impassive, never looking at him, intent upon her knitting. He reproaches her for leaving him without a word, assuring her at the same time that he makes no reproaches. He admits that he wanted her to leave, but he knows now what it is to do without her. She is his heart and soul and the "failings" of his soul.

I gave you my body and my soul, my soul to do with as you wish. My soul as if it were mine, you took, as if you knew what it was and what it is used for. And if I made you go away, you know it had to be. You said so yourself, for Ciz was away and we would have fixed everything up. Then there would have been only a few months and I would have joined you. . . . But now I am telling you Ciz is dead and I can take you for my wife. (III,98–99)

Still Ysé says nothing. Mesa refuses to believe that her love for him is over. He wants to take her back, to take her and the child to safety. He has on him a safe-conduct that everyone will respect. Amalric returns. Mesa pulls out a revolver, but Amalric wrests it from him, and in a violent fight throws him to the ground. Ysé has not moved. Unmoving still, she says with a strange voice: "Murderer!"

They take his pass and his money and they prepare to go. "He'll blow up instead of us. The time bomb is set." Ysé protests, but ends up by insisting only that they do not leave him on the floor all crumpled up. Amalric obliges by getting a large Chinese armchair with a round back "in the form of Omega," but stands by while Ysé struggles alone to put him in it. What of the child? "He is dead," Ysé says, returning from the other room. Earlier, we learned that he was very sick. Ysé apparently has finished him off. They leave Mesa, solemnly installed in his chair, "arrayed to face the events."

For Claudel, everything in the world speaks with its own voice. One must learn how to listen. "As time passes between us," Ysé had said to Mesa on the boat, "it makes a tiny crackling sound." Now, in the ruins of the Confucian temple, "the noise of the stars, for they do make a noise, as all those who have troubled to listen know," is expressed by a low rumbling, sometimes weak, sometimes strong, like that of a distant liturgy: "Quis est iste involvens sententias verbis imperitis?" Words that Job heard from the heart of the whirlwind.

Mesa has slowly recovered consciousness, accompanied "by a rinforzando of the stellar kettle."

> Why? *(Muffled explanation of the kettle)* Why she? Why that woman suddenly on the boat, with such skill, and at that moment? What did she have to do with me? Did I need her? *(The kettle pretends not to hear and is occupied with something else.)* It was you alone! (III,107)

Mesa rushes on, accusing the Voice of "pulling tricks" and making "clever moves." When the kettle tries to answer,

Mesa interrupts. "Just don't talk, so there will be a way of hearing you." The kettle is not pleased and manages to get in a word edgewise: "The others." What does it mean? The kettle, "in its immense language distributed over the entire firmament," repeats:

> The others—the others—the others—the others. The others, for better or for worse, exist, and not just you alone. Have you finally learned that? (III,109)

Yes, Mesa has learned it. He needed someone "with her face" to teach him, and no one else. If that was what God didn't know and needed to learn, then, yes, it was worth the trouble to create the world, and "the cross wasn't anything superfluous." Mesa loved her, and she ran away.

> It is not with kisses and biting that you succeed, it is with the cross. An instrument which You are watching me slowly build. (III,110)

And once the cross "has begun to function like any other instrument," can Mesa resist it? He must love Ysé now *by way of* the cross; must make his renunciation complete and commend into the hands of God her soul, which he won at the expense of his own. In losing her he will find her. And when he finds her she will speak his name, that name "which she alone knows."

Ysé returns to die with Mesa. The boat on which she and Amalric were to have escaped was swept away. "I heard only one cry in the night. A kind of ridiculous cry." And now Mesa's "huge boat" returns to him on the tide of midnight, to carry him into the open sea of the love of God. "It isn't easy," Mesa had said, "to run away from God," to run away from the million stars that "were mounting guard over her." She sits beside him in the chair shaped like an Omega: "The two pincers," she says, "have closed over us and we are caught." Caught by Him who is the Alpha and the Omega.

"Mesa, I am Ysé." That is why she tried to escape from him. But at that very moment the stars hit her "square in the face, like a sunstroke."

YSÉ: What are they up to, Mesa, in their uselessness, those stars in the sky?
MESA: What do you mean?
YSÉ: There had to be someone, I guess, to give me all those useless stars.
MESA: I can't unhook them for you.
YSÉ: It's easy. Just stretch out your hand. (III,120)

She takes his hand and forces him to get up. Then, "as if it were a work difficult to accomplish," she raises his hand with great care. He stands erect, while she sinks down at his feet in the dark, saying:

Remember me for one moment in this darkness, I was once your vine.

Mesa is the one that shall unhook all the stars for her, but she is the vine by which he reaches them. His raised hand, luminous with desire, is the last image to fill "the hollow of the stage."[11]

In *Partage de Midi,* as in *The Cocktail Party,* but with a passion never felt in the latter play, man reaches out for a fulfillment that cannot be had *in,* but may be had partly *through,* personal relationships, especially the love between man and woman. Even if it is a sinful relationship. Mesa "yields up his spirit" on the cross that is Ysé, just as Celia died to Edward. But Mesa, having found God through Ysé, finds Ysé in God, his love for her now purified and transfigured.

NOTES

[1] In the introduction to the translation used throughout this chapter (Chicago: Henry Regnery, Gateway Edition, 1960), Wallace Fowlie explains that he rejected "Divide of Noon" as too peaceful for the dramatic connotation of the French title, *Partage de Midi.* "The French word *midi* denotes time and place and passion" (p. xii). The meaning of this word is implied in the very names of the characters. As Claudel explained in an interview: "Ysé, in Greek, is equality, *isos, isé,* it means equal. Mesa, that's half. Amalric, phonetically, you have to cut into two. It's the name of an umbrella shop in the Boulevard Magenta, Amalric: [evidently changing his mind] it's divided into three. And finally, De Ciz, it's a clean cut" (P. Claudel and J. Amrouche, *Mémoires improvisés,* chap. 25 [Paris: Gallimard, 1954], quoted in *Principles of Tragedy,* by Geoffrey Brereton [Coral Gables, Fla.: University of Miami Press, 1968], p. 231).

[2] *Oeuvres complètes, théâtre,* vol. 11 (Gallimard, 1957), p. 307. It is common knowledge that the drama of the first two acts is autobiographical. Henri Peyre notes that the woman who becomes Ysé was a Polish countess who lived long enough to attend the first performance of the play in 1948. Claudel married another woman at the bidding of his confessor, and they adopted the child that was born of his affair with the countess ("A Dramatist of Genius," *Chicago Review* XV [Autumn, 1961]: 74, 76). Writing to André Gide on March 3, 1908, only a few years after "the noon of his life," Claudel has a sure sense of the road he travels by: "The joy of this 40th year which we are both traversing is precisely what I call the *happiness of responsibility,* the profound satisfaction of knowing that so many hearts are resting upon your own, that so many hands are clasping ours, and the sense that we shan't let them down, that we are in possession of the truth and are contributing to the solidarity of the universe. None of the intoxication of passion can replace this deep feeling of brotherhood" (*The Correspondence 1899–1926 between Paul Claudel and André Gide,* prefaced and translated by John Russell [London: Secker & Warburg, 1952], p. 73).

[3] Press release, 8 December 1948, *Oeuvres complètes,* 11, p. 305.

[4] Wallace Fowlie notes in his Introduction that *le demon du midi* is a phrase coined by Paul Bourget to describe carnality. Actually, the phrase itself, apart from any meaning one might attach to it, is a translation of the *daemonium meridianum* as it appears in verse six of psalm 90 (91) of the Latin Vulgate, rendered into the

English of the old Douay translation as "the noonday devil." This psalm, in both scripture and liturgy, is associated with Christ's temptation in the desert at the end of forty days.

[5] *The Satin Slipper,* trans. the Rev. John O'Connor with the collaboration of the author (New Haven: Yale University Press, 1931), The Third Day, sc. 8, p. 172.

[6] In an informal discussion at the Yale School of Drama, May 12, 1969, Jean-Louis Barrault spoke eloquently of the singular power of Claudel's words to evoke the act of love. What is even more remarkable is Claudel's ability to portray the erotic with a passion that greatly expands the dramatic experience without ever escaping it.

[7] *Le Drame de Paul Claudel* (Paris: Desclée, 1936), p. 64.

[8] *Les Nouvelles littéraires,* 15 November 1951, reprinted in *Regards sur le théâtre de Claudel* (Paris: Beauchesne, 1964), p. 132.

[9] *Le Soulier de satin* (Paris: Club du Meilleur Livre, 1953), Appendix, p. 20, quoted in Guicharnaud, *Modern French Theatre,* rev. ed. (New Haven: Yale University Press, 1967), p. 73.

[10] *Oeuvres complètes,* 1, *Corona Benignitatis Anni Dei, "Images et Signets entre les feuillets"* (Paris: Gallimard, 1915). My translation.

[11] Throughout this chapter I refer only to the "nouvelle version" published by Claudel in 1949. In earlier versions, the language of the ending was much more lyrical. "It was Wagner before," Barrault said in a discussion at Yale, "then it was Beethoven." When I asked him if in later productions he had ever used the "Beethoven" ending, he said no, because he remained convinced that the whole thrust of the play demanded the more lyrical ending. Claudel's concern was that no word be heard except in dialogue with the "immense language" of the stars.

VI. CAMINO REAL

I

Like Claudel in *Partage de Midi,* Williams in *Camino Real* takes up the lives of his characters when the sun, irrevocably, begins its downward course. The first verse of Dante's *Inferno* serves as epigraph to the play:

> In the middle of the journey of our life
> I came to myself in a dark wood
> where the straight way was lost.

But "the middle of the journey" is not the same for all the characters on the Camino Real. The legendary Jacques Casanova is in "his late middle years." Marguerite Gautier, "a beautiful woman of indefinite age," always wears a white camellia now, "but there used to be five evenings out of the month when a pink camellia, instead of the usual white one, let my admirers know that the moon those nights was unfavorable to pleasure, and so they called me—Camille." Kilroy, the main character, is "a young American vagrant, about twenty-seven." But he has been prematurely brought to the middle of his journey: He has a bad heart, so bad that he had to retire from the prize ring, and give up liquor and smoking and sex.

The dark wood into which Kilroy stumbles is the plaza of a walled town in an unspecified Latin American country. The map of the place carries a warning reminiscent of the inscription cut in stone over the Gate of

Dante's Hell: "Turn back, Traveler, for the spring of humanity has gone dry in this place. . . ."[1] For here the Ca*m*ino Re*al* comes to an end and the *Ca*mino *Re*al begins.

If one expresses "Camino Real" in English, that means "the way of reality." If one expresses it in Spanish, then it means "Royal Road" . . . the road of the Spanish knights who conquered the land, but also the road upon which Christianity came to the West Coast of America.[2]

The missionary stations, represented by the sixteen blocks into which the play is divided, "lay upon this way, a day's journey from one another. . . . Today, however, the old missionary way has become a street of industry, of money, of tourist trade—a business reality."

From another point of view, *Ca*mino *Re*al becomes again Ca*m*ino Re*al*. In Chapter Twelve, "Of the Royal Way of the Cross," of *The Imitation of Christ*, Book Two, we read what Kilroy comes to discover:

> Arrange all things to your liking, yet you shall always find something to suffer, whether you will it or not; and thus you always find the cross.
>
> For you shall either feel pain of body, or suffer tribulation of spirit.
>
> At times you will be forsaken by God; and at times you will be tried by your neighbor; and what is more, you will often be a burden to your own self.[3]

Kilroy's Way of the Cross takes him, as it took Jesus, through fourteen stations (his entrance marks the beginning of the third of the sixteen blocks). As a movement of the spirit, his journey can be expressed in a line from the Christian Creed: He descended into hell, the third day he rose again from the dead. Kilroy's three days are compressed into one, but that one day is as long as a man's dream, not to be measured by the time it takes. The dreamer is Don Quixote, who appears in the Prologue and then again at the end. Sancho has left him, heeding the warning on the map. The day is about to dawn. "I'll sleep and dream for a while against the wall of this town," Quixote says. "And tomorrow at this same hour . . . I will go on from here with a new companion and this old bit of blue ribbon to keep me in mind of distance that I have gone and distance I have yet to go."

II

The stage directions require that a phoenix painted on silk be softly lighted now and then in the play, because "resurrections are so much a part of its meaning." And for every resurrection there is, of course, a death, a diminishment. There are diminishments whose origin lies within the characters, and diminishments whose origin lies outside them.[4] For Kilroy, the internal diminishment of first importance is his weak heart, "a heart as big as the head of a baby." Because of his heart he had to leave the street "when the street was royal":

> My real true woman, my wife, she would of stuck with me, but it was all spoiled with her being scared and me, too, that a real hard kiss would kill me!—So one night while she was sleeping I wrote her good-bye . . . (Block III)

Because of his heart he is in constant fear of the Streetcleaners, two men in dirty white jackets who periodically trundle a white barrel across the plaza. Kilroy sees what the barrel is for when he witnesses the fate of a character called the Survivor.

The Survivor, one of several young explorers who had attempted to cross the desert, the "Terra Incognita," has come back, dying of thirst. But the public fountains have gone dry. La Madrecita, a blind singer led by a ragged young man called the Dreamer, cradles the dying man in her arms "in the attitude of a Pietà." Her compassion is the first "resurrection" on the Camino Real, and it foreshadows the service she will render Kilroy at the end of the play. The Dreamer expresses his compassion in a word: *Hermano,* brother, "the most dangerous word in the human language." So says Gutman, a town official and owner of the Siete Mares Hotel. The word is dangerous because it incites the people to riot. The Survivor ceases to survive, and Kilroy looks on in horror while the two Streetcleaners stuff his body into the barrel and wheel him away. Death, this death, stands at the very beginning of the play as an image of all the partial "deaths" or diminishments that are yet to come:

> Death is the sum and consummation of all our diminishments: it is *evil* itself—purely physical evil, in so far as it results organically in the manifold structure of that physical nature in which we are immersed—but a moral evil too, insofar as in the society to which we belong, or in ourselves, the wrong use of our freedom, by spreading disorder, converts the manifold complexity of our nature into the source of all evil and all corruption.[5]

The first external diminishment that Kilroy suffers on the Camino Real is the loss of all his money. When he protests to a lounging officer that he has been robbed, he is told that he never had any money, he was just dreaming. He is forced to hock something. His golden gloves? Never! The silver-framed photo of his One True Woman? Never! He settles at last on his ruby-and-emerald-studded belt with the word CHAMP on it. But the loan shark isn't interested, he wants the gloves. Kilroy is adamant: "I'd hustle my heart on this street, I'd peddle my heart's true blood before I'd ever leave my golden gloves hung up in a loan shark's window." Still penniless, he emerges into the plaza where he encounters the Streetcleaners again. Doubled up in their barrel is the Baron de Charlus, an elderly sybarite who had been on the prowl for a young man but had passed Kilroy by because his eyes were "too gentle for someone who has as much as I to atone for." As the Streetcleaners wheel him by, they point and snicker at Kilroy.

At this point, Kilroy meets Jacques Casanova. "What do they do with a stiff picked up in this town?" he asks. Affecting nonchalance for the benefit of the watching guards, Jacques explains the disposition of the bodies: If the pockets are empty, as his own happen to be, the "stiff" is wheeled straight to the Laboratory. "And there the individual becomes an undistinguished member of a collectivist state." His chemical components are sorted out and vital organs or parts, if unique in size or structure, are preserved in formaldehyde and placed on exhibition. It is not very romantic, to say the least. And romance is important, they both agree on that.

KILROY: We're buddies under the skin!
JACQUES: Travelers born?
KILROY: Always looking for something!
JACQUES: Satisfied by nothing!
KILROY: Hopeful?
JACQUES: Always!

(V)

It is another "resurrection," a rising of spirits to meet in fraternal understanding. But is there no way off the Camino, Kilroy asks, no way out? The Way Out, Casanova replies, is up that steep ramp and through that archway, the "Magnificent Arch of Triumph." Without hesitation Kilroy plunges up almost to the top, then stops abruptly. The desert wind sings loudly.

> I don't see nothing but nothing—and then more nothing. And then I see some mountains. But the mountains are covered with snow. (V)

The "traveler born" turns back: "Maybe sometime with someone but not right now and alone." Casanova can't go because he is "sweetly encumbered" with a lady. Or so he hopes.

Kilroy, left alone, looks for a room. But money is the only thing that speaks on the Camino Real. Disconsolate, he turns away, and is granted another small resurrection of spirit: La Madrecita, crouched near the dry fountain, offers him some food. But she cannot save him from the next diminishment: Gutman has him arrested for vagrancy. When he protests that he was robbed, Gutman calls for witnesses, but the only one present who would have raised her voice for him is blind. Kilroy is declared to be a Patsy and tossed a red fright wig, a big crimson nose that lights up and clown pants with a huge footprint on the seat.

He blinks an S.O.S. to Casanova on his red bulb nose. Casanova had been afraid that something of this sort would happen:

> You have a spark of anarchy in your spirit and that's not to be tolerated. Nothing wild or honest is tolerated here! It has to be extinguished or used only to light up your nose for Mr. Gutman's amusement. . . . Before the final block we'll find some way out of here! Meanwhile, patience and courage, little brother! (VII)

Marguerite now commands Jacques' attention. She, too, has been robbed—of her purse with her passport and all her papers. Fortunately, she still has her jewels. But Jacques is embarrassed when she has to pay for the wine that he has ordered. When she inquires about the letter he has been expecting, he answers that it came this morning but he hasn't had the nerve to open it. His reason is the same as the Stranger's in *Till Damaskus:* "I've had so many unpleasant surprises that I've lost faith in my luck."[6]

At the moment Jacques is not lucky at love either. Marguerite still prefers young lovers to him. And she is desperate to leave the Camino Real. She berates him for not helping her:

> You really don't want to leave here. You *think* you don't want to go because you're brave as an old hawk. But the truth of the matter—the real not the royal truth—is that you're terrified of the Terra Incognita outside that wall. (VII)

He admits it; he is terrified of "the unknown country inside or outside this wall or any place on earth without you with me."

What is this Terra Incognita? The party of young explorers, of which the Survivor was a member, tried to cross it and all perished. Kilroy took one look at it and backed away. Now Jacques admits his terror of it. Lord Byron, who emerges from the Siete Mares prepared for departure, brings us closer to an answer. He reminisces about the death of Shelley, the cremation of his body, the snatching of his heart when the ribs unlocked.

> I thought it was a disgusting thing to do, to snatch a man's heart from his body! What can one man do with another man's heart? (VIII)

Kilroy knows, Jacques knows. The "Great Lover" seizes a loaf of bread and twists it and tears it, stamps on it and kicks it away. "But a poet's vocation," says Lord Byron, "which used to be my vocation, is to influence the heart in a gentler fashion than you have made your mark on that loaf of bread." He was seduced away from that vocation. Now he will go in search of it again. He will do what he must: *"Make voyages!—Attempt them!*—there's nothing else. . . ." And he goes, into the desert, believing that his spirit will stretch across it. Kilroy, catching fire, plunges after him—but loses his nerve and sits, blinking his nose.

III

There are two major events in the play that can only be regarded as "false resurrections." The first is the nonscheduled flight of the Fugitivo, the second the "restoration" of virginity to Esmeralda, the Gypsy's daughter.

Without warning, the Fugitivo lands near the northwest corner of the plaza. Not even Gutman had been informed that it was coming. Its arrival is the signal for pandemonium, in the root sense of the word. People rush about like demons, desperate to secure a seat, on the one hand, and their possessions, on the other. Lord and Lady Mulligan are a case in point. The Lady is especially good at shoving. When her husband lags behind, suddenly sick, she forbids him to be sick until they get on the plane. Two men, dressed in swallowtails, rush to Lord Mulligan's side. Lady Mulligan screams: "The Streetcleaners!" She leaves her husband to their mercy, calling back as she goes: "Pack Lord Mulligan's body in dry ice! Ship Air Express to Cobh care of Mulligan Iron & Steel Works, in Cobh!"

Marguerite is no less frantic. But for her the atmosphere assumes the density of a dream. She can't get through. This time money is not enough, she must have papers.

MARGUERITE: Jacques! He wants my papers! Give him my papers, Jacques!
JACQUES: The lady's papers are lost!
MARGUERITE: No, no, no, THAT IS NOT TRUE! HE

WANTS TO KEEP ME HERE! HE'S LYING ABOUT IT! (IX)

It is noteworthy that Jacques himself makes no attempt to board the plane. Nor does Kilroy, who occupies himself during this episode by "trying to make a fast buck or two as a Redcap." The motive behind Casanova's attitude—and perhaps Kilroy's, for they are brothers at heart—must be the very motive for which Marguerite had mocked him earlier: He does not want to leave until he can leave with honor. There is no honor to be found in the conduct of the boarding passengers: They are inhuman with the inhumanity of the Camino Real. Their flight can only be a "false resurrection," and indeed, we learn later that the Fugitivo has crashed in Elizabeth, New Jersey.

The second "false resurrection"—the restoration of virginity to Esmeralda, the Gypsy's daughter—occurs during the festivities of the Camino's carnival. Esmeralda is a reluctant "virgin." Earlier, when Kilroy tried to escape, she tried to escape with him, but the Gypsy, with the help of her accomplices, dragged her back to captivity. Now the proud mother proclaims the good news: The moon has restored her daughter's virginity:

ESMERALDA! RISE WITH THE MOON, MY DAUGHTER! CHOOSE THE HERO! (XI)

The stage directions indicate that the fiesta is a sort of serio-comic, grotesque-lyric "Rites of Fertility" with roots in various pagan cultures. What it says in the play is a parody of what such rites were supposed to say in pagan cultures. Mircea Eliade, speaking from the primitive's "lunar perspective," explains:

Everything begins over again at its commencement every instant. The past is but a prefiguration of the future. No event is irreversible and no transformation is final.[7]

In the context of the Camino Real, this is to say that there is no hope, no way out except in the barrel of the Streetcleaners, and that the past is the pattern of the future. Esmeralda's "virginity," in its offer to "begin again," serves to tempt the Chosen Hero, and traps him.

Kilroy, naturally, is the Chosen Hero. The honor comes to him just as he is about to put into effect his plan to escape. Disguised in turban, dark gloves and burnoose, he emerges from the pawnshop, having hocked his golden gloves. With a cross (Casanova's gift) clasped in his hands, he is preparing to leap over the wall when Esmeralda spots him: "Hero! Champ!"

KILROY: I'm not in condition!
ESMERALDA: You're still the Champ, the undefeated Champ of the golden gloves!
KILROY: Nobody's called me that in a long, long time!
ESMERALDA: Champ!
KILROY: My resistance is crumbling!
ESMERALDA: Champ!
KILROY: It's crumbled!
ESMERALDA: Hero!
KILROY: GERONIMO! (XI)

He is caught. After he has lifted her spangled veil, he says, "It wasn't much to give my golden gloves for."

ESMERALDA: You pity yourself?
KILROY: That's right, I pity myself and everybody that goes to the Gypsy's daughter. I pity the world and I pity the God who made it. (XII)

IV

Kilroy and Jacques must each suffer two more diminishments before the final "resurrection." Marguerite is the instrument of Casanova's penultimate diminishment, and in the process she brings about her own. She sends word to a "charming young man" that she is bored with her present company, that she missed the Fugitivo and wants to forget she missed it. That night at the fiesta the deserted Casanova is crowned with "a crown of horns," and hailed "the King of Cuckolds on the Camino Real." Later, Marguerite suffers her own diminishment at the hands of her young lover. He strips her of jewels and cloak, rips her dress and frisks her for anything else she might have of value. "What else do I have that you want?" And the young man answers contemptuously: "Nothing."

Jacques suffers his last diminishment when, under threat of eviction from the Siete Mares, he finally gets up nerve enough to open his letter. Remittances? No, remittances discontinued. Gutman throws him out, portmanteau going before him. "And so at last it has come, the distinguished thing!"

Kilroy, for his part, prepares himself for the last stages of his descent into hell. His big heart was beating furiously when he lifted Esmeralda's veil, and now he tells Casanova that "the altitude on this block has affected my ticker." Breathing heavily, he climbs to the top of the ramp and stands looking out at Terra Incognita. He hears the piping of the Streetcleaners and challenges them when they appear: "COME ON, YOU SONS OF BITCHES! KILROY IS HERE! HE'S READY!" He swings at them wildly, then finally collapses. Just as they are about to pounce, La Madrecita covers his body with her shawl.

She cradles him as she had cradled the Survivor, in the attitude of a Pietà. While the Laboratory personnel prepare to dissect the body of a "sheeted figure" stretched out on a table nearby, she says over the body cradled in her lap: "This was thy son, America—and now mine." She sings his praises: "His heart was pure gold and as big as the head of a baby." Then, touching his face with flowers: "Rise, ghost! Go! Go, bird! 'Humankind cannot bear very much reality.' " He rises like a phoenix—only to discover that the Laboratory personnel are also interested in the size and quality of his heart. Snatching up the golden sphere removed from the "corpse" on their table, Kilroy flees with it down the aisle, in a "dream-like re-enactment" of his earlier escape attempt.

KILROY: This is my heart! It don't belong to no State, not even the U.S.A. Which way is out? Where's the Greyhound depot? Nobody's going to put my heart in a bottle in a museum and charge admission to support the rotten police! Where are they? Which way are they going? Or coming? Hey, somebody, help me get out of here! Which way do I—which way—which way do I—*go! go! go! go! go! Gee, I'm lost! I don't know where I am!* I'm all turned around, I'm *confused,* I don't understand—what's—happened, it's like a—*dream,* it's —just like a—dream . . . *Mary! Oh, Mary! Mary! Mary, help a Christian!! Help a Christian, Mary!*—It's like a dream. . . .
(XVI)

In his confusion and desperation, he makes one last attempt to escape: It proves to be a repetition of the "false resurrection" he had suffered earlier at the hands of Esmeralda and he falls all the harder into the hell of his diminishments. Having flung the Mary prayer into the thick atmosphere of his dream, he overhears Esmeralda fling a prayer of her own:

God bless all con men and hustlers and pitch-men who hawk their hearts on the street, all two-time losers who're likely to lose once more, the courtesan who made the mistake of love, the greatest of lovers crowned with the longest horns, the poet who wandered far from his heart's green country and possibly will and possibly won't be able to find his way back, look down with a smile tonight on the last cavaliers, the ones with rusty armor and soiled white plumes, and visit with understanding and something that's almost tender those fading legends that come and go in this plaza like songs not clearly remembered, oh, sometime and somewhere, let there be something to mean the word *honor* again! (XVI)

Esmeralda, in her "childish nightgown," says her prayer out of the languor of her heart. But Quixote, waking at last from his dream, cries out a lusty *Amen!* And Kilroy echoes it, even as Esmeralda's last sleepy prayer drifts into his ears: *"And, oh, God, let me dream tonight of the Chosen Hero! . . .* The *only* one, *Kilroy! He was sincere!"* Believing her, he rushes to her window, heart in hand. "Go away, cat." What can he do "to convince this doll" that he is real? He trades in his golden heart for jewels, furs and sequined gowns. But still it is "Go away, cat. . . ." Esmeralda falls asleep. Kilroy rushes to the Gypsy's door and pounds on it with both fists. For his trouble he gets the contents of a slop-jar thrown into his face. "Had for a button! Stewed, screwed, and tattooed on the Camino Real!"

Quixote approaches the fountain. It begins to flow! Kilroy falls back in amazement.

QUIXOTE: Have you got any plans?
KILROY: Well, I was thinking of—going *on* from—*here!*
QUIXOTE: Good! Come with me. (XVI)

The old dreamer has found his companion. The fountain is flowing loudly and sweetly now. People begin to move toward it with murmurs of wonder. Marguerite comes forward, then Casanova. She extends a pleading hand toward him. He hesitates, then comes to her side, and with a low cry she seizes his hand and presses it to her lips. Quixote cries out powerfully from the archway leading out to the mountains across the desert: *"The violets in the moun-*

tains have broken the rocks!" and goes out with Kilroy at his side.

V

The violets in the mountains. On Block Ten, just before Marguerite had left Casanova for her young lover, she said to him: "Tenderness, the violets in the mountains—can't break the rocks!" And Casanova had answered: "The violets in the mountains can break the rocks if you believe in them and allow them to grow!"

But Jacques, alone, could not muster faith enough. It was Don Quixote's faith, great enough to leap across the desert, purer than Lord Byron's, that made the violets in the mountains grow and break the rocks and set the water flowing again. Tenderness, honor, love—these thrusts of humanity must make themselves felt again if the *Ca*mino *Re*al is to become the Ca*m*i*no* Re*al*. But this they cannot do—without courage, faith, hope. Insofar as one life-view is supported by another, perhaps it is not too farfetched to say that the relationship of Marguerite and Jacques to Kilroy and Quixote at the end of the play is the relationship of Edward and Lavinia Chamberlayne to Celia Coplestone at the end of *The Cocktail Party*.

Here, too, is the main weakness of Williams' play. Celia, and then Edward and Lavinia, come to realize that they are all somehow involved in the wrongs of society. But Kilroy, and Marguerite and Jacques, are too much the romantic victims. Is it enough to say, as Quixote says to Kilroy, *"Don't! Pity! Your! Self!"*? Responsibility for evil is not denied in the play, but it is not adverted to. Such is not always the case among Williams' anti-heroes, to use a term ably explored by Esther Merle Jackson in her book on Williams' "broken world." Kilroy, with Brick, Chance, Blanche, Shannon, are "images of a humanity diminished by time and history."[8] But Kilroy stands apart from these other protagonists: Like them, he is "in search of his identity in the universe," but unlike them, he is not "in flight from the consequences of his own transgressions." Or, if he is, he is not aware of it, and neither are we.

In his descent into hell, Kilroy pushes toward resurrection, though the symbolic elements of the play never converge upon the mystery of this term. "As far as we know," Williams once wrote, "as far as there exists any kind of empiric evidence, there is no way to beat the game of *being* against *non-being,* in which non-being is the predestined victor on realistic levels."[9] But *Camino Real* moves not on realistic levels but on the level of dream. For Kilroy, to push toward resurrection is to go on playing, precisely in the hope of beating the game of being against non-being.

NOTES

[1] Tennessee Williams, *Camino Real.* Copyright 1948, 1953 by Tennessee Williams. Reprinted by permission of New Directions Publishing Corporation. All Rights Reserved.

[2] *Bochumer Diskussion über "Camino Real" von Tennessee Williams* (Frankfurt-am-Main, 1955), p. 8, quoted in *The Broken World of Tennessee Williams* by Esther Merle Jackson (Madison, Milwaukee & London: University of Wisconsin Press, 1966), p. 121.

[3] The translation is that of Joseph Malaise, S.J., *The Following of Christ* (New York: America Press, 1937), p. 107.

[4] I use here a distinction made by Pierre Teilhard de Chardin in *The Divine Milieu* (New York: Harper Torchbooks, 1955), pp. 81–82.

[5] *The Divine Milieu,* p. 82.

[6] This is only one of several affinities with Strindberg's pilgrimage plays. During a Stockholm interview (mentioned by Richard B. Vowles in his article "Tennessee Williams and Strindberg," *Modern Drama* I [December, 1958], pp. 166–71), Williams explicitly denied the influence of Strindberg, which makes the affinities all the more

remarkable. Among the affinities that Vowles cites are the structure of *Camino Real* to that of *The Great Highway,* described by Strindberg as "A Drama of a Pilgrimage, with Seven Road Stops," and the removal of Kilroy's golden heart to the excision of the father's heart in *Lucky Per's Journey.*

[7] *Cosmos and History,* p. 89.

[8] *The Broken World of Tennessee Williams,* chap. 4.

[9] "The Timeless World of a Play," published with *The Rose Tattoo* (New York: New Directions, 1951).

VII. HUNGER AND THIRST

I

"You're never satisfied," says Marie-Madeleine to her husband Jean, and that's the long and the short of it. When they lived in the new building with "windows everywhere," Jean complained that there was too much space. Now that they've returned to the old basement, he complains that it's unhealthy: "Mud everywhere!" He admits that "looking forward to something" is all that keeps him going; he only lives "in the hope that something out of the ordinary will turn up." He is not content with peace, he must have "boundless joy and ecstasy." He has a great place in his heart for Marie-Madeleine and their baby, Marthe, but "the universe is greater," and what he lacks is "greater still." So miserable is he in his hunger and thirst that he cries out: "I can't bear my own existence!"

Ionesco has said that there is in Jean "a little bit of Faust."[1] In this, Jean is one with humanity. And yet Marie berates him for not living "like everybody else." In what way is he not like everybody else? Marie, apparently—and in her opinion, everybody else—has quieted the Faust in her soul. As a woman, she perhaps knows better how to contain him. For her, it's all in the way you look at things. "These walls," she says, "with their stains of damp and mildew, have you ever really seen them?" Where Jean sees vertebrae dripping blood, heads weighed down with sorrow, bodies without heads and arms, she sees islands and ancient cities, friendly faces and hands extended in welcome. "Old houses are full of moving memories," she says, and one of them promptly enters from the left: Aunt Adelaide, "a great lady in decline." It seems that Aunt Adelaide died in a fire, and in the fire of his dreamworld Jean always sees her holding out her arms to him, in agony, "like a reproach."[2]

But Marie assures him that her death wasn't his fault. The faces of the past are kind, she insists.

> Dead relatives and friends, if made to live again, make agreeable companions. They're a world in themselves. Turn the shadows of the past into a night full of repose. The present is all sunshine, if you want it to be; the future, clear and bright. If your vision's good, you can see through walls. The walls will no longer hide the horizon. . . . Make every setback a time for rest, for *détente*. In the morning, look forward to the peace of evening: it will come. At night, dream of the festival of the dawn. That too will come. In this way, all is achieved.[3]

Jean rejects her solution outright. It is "chimerical, impossible!" But for all her naïveté, it is Marie who poses the main question of the play: "Where does he want to go in order to find what he already has in hand? Where else will he find it but here?" (I,95). But go he does, literally wrenching from his heart a branch of the wild-rose, *sans grimacer,* and tossing it down on the table. Marie finds it there, *la fleur d'amour,* and mourns. At that moment the back wall disappears, and she sees a garden: trees in bloom, tall green grass, a very blue sky and a silver ladder hanging in the air. She cries out:

> He didn't know *that* was here! He couldn't have seen *that!* I had a feeling the garden was here; I suspected it. I myself wasn't absolutely sure. If only he could have seen, if only he could have known, if only he had had a little patience. . . .
> (I,103)

It is an old story, older surely than *Peer Gynt* or *The Blue Bird.* Mircea Eliade tells of a pious rabbi, Eisik of Cracow, who left his home to find a hidden treasure. Three times he had dreamed that it lay buried beneath the great bridge in Prague. There he met an officer, who asked him, kindly, if he had lost something. When the rabbi recounted his dream, the officer burst into laughter, for he too had heard voices in the night. Had he been foolish enough to heed them, he would have gone to Cracow to look for a great treasure in the house of a certain rabbi named Eisik. The rabbi thanked him and returned to Cracow. There, buried behind the stove, he found the treasure.

> Thus, the real treasure . . . is never very far; there is no need to seek it in a distant country. It lies buried in the most intimate parts of our own house; that is, of our own being. It is behind the stove, the centre of the life and warmth that rule our existence, the heart of our heart, if only we know how to unearth it. And yet—there is this strange and persistent fact, that it is only after a pious journey in a distant region, in a new land, that the meaning of that inner voice guiding us on our search can make itself understood by us. And to this strange and persistent fact is added another: that he who reveals to us the meaning of our mysterious inward pilgrimage must himself be a stranger, of another belief and another race.[4]

By the end of the first episode, entitled "The Flight," we know clearly, if symbolically, where Jean will find the treasure that his heart desires: in his own home, with his own wife and child, in the garden "behind the stove," with the silver ladder suspended from on high. The trouble is, *he* doesn't know it, and he will not believe his wife; he must hear it from strangers. He must go into distant lands, searching for what lies hidden in his own house, and we must go with him, through two more episodes, through ideals ("The Rendezvous") and ideologies ("The Black Masses of the Good Inn").

II

Her eyes are "the color of certain dreams." In trying to describe the lady he is waiting for, Jean is never able to get much more specific than that. He waits on "a terrace that appears to be hanging in mid-air," surrounded by "arid mountains" and bathed in a cold brilliance, "without shadow, without sun." He is alone, except for the two caretakers of the "museum" at whose entrance he is waiting. He has been here before—yes, of course, he has—and that's why he has come back, after traveling through dark and rainy lands. Northern lands? He's not quite sure, he has no sense of direction. But this—this is "the kingdom of light."

"A bit bleak, this light," the First Caretaker says, "and rather brittle. But if it meets with your approval, take your fill of it."

Strictly speaking, Jean is happy now because, as he says, he knows he *will* be happy when the lady gets here. "Hope, well-founded expectation, that's what makes me happy" (II,107). Which sounds very much like the advice he rejected. "Drink from the cup of hope," Marie had said, "and you will never be thirsty" (I,94). And then she had launched into the speech already quoted. The word *speech* is apt: Marie's "hope" sounds too much like "optimism," and the optimist is essentially a maker of speeches.

> The optimist, as such, always relies upon an experience which is not drawn from the most intimate and living part of himself, but, on the contrary, is *considered from a sufficient distance* to

allow certain contradictions to become alternated or fused into a general harmony.[5]

Jean, however, will claim that his "hope" is not like that at all; in fact, he makes it synonymous with "well-founded expectation":

"I'll come for sure," she said. She couldn't have made that promise lightly, could she? She said again: "I'll come for sure. Even if I lose my memory, it will still be me; if you forget, it will still be you; it will still be us, but without our memories." Lose one's memory? We arranged to meet again in the month of June, at eleven o'clock. At three in the afternoon? On the fifteenth? The thirteenth? The seventeenth? Or was it in July? (II,110)

Such is his "well-founded expectation." What Jean has done, of course, is to project, out of his dreams, the ideal woman.

JEAN: I don't want one of those women who all look alike and who look like her.
FIRST CARETAKER: You're fussy.
JEAN: I want the one whom all the others look like, not one of those who look like her. (II,116)

She is "a chapel on the top of a hill, a temple that looms suddenly in the virgin forest—no, she is herself the forest—she is hill, valley, clearing" (II,109). She will teach him the meaning of joy and will wake in him a zest for living such as he has never known before. All the years he's wasted, she will give them back to him. She is "absolute necessity" (II,117).

Having made such a projection, he sets the time and place for his rendezvous with her, thus setting the time and place for his undoing. For what he does is to identify the rendezvous with redemption. He says, in effect, that everything is lost if she does not come. Implicitly, he tells himself that if his expectations are not fulfilled, according to the conditions he has set, he will have no possibility of escaping from the despair into which he must inevitably sink.[6]

I have looked for fulfillment and all I find is torment. I had the choice between peace and passion. I chose passion, fool that I was. And yet there I was in my shelter, securely enclosed in my gloom, in my nostalgia, in my fears, in my remorse, in my anguish, in my responsibilities, there in my shelter, surrounded, as it were, by so many protecting walls. The fear of death was my surest protection. Now the walls have crumbled, and here I am, open to attack. The walls have crumbled, and here I am in the scorching hell of life, in the throbbing despair of my misery. (II,114)

One word would suffice to save him, he thinks. But who can speak it? Surely not the caretakers, but at Jean's request they pretend to pity him, wiping their eyes and blowing their noses. Waiting is the action of this episode, as it is in *Waiting for Godot,* but unlike Estragon and Vladimir, Jean has not reached the point of immobility. He goes off, crying for the lady to lighten his darkness, to answer his hunger and thirst. His flight expresses the same desperation as their immobility, in much the same way as brashness, in one person, and shyness, in another, express the same fear.

Before they go their separate ways, the Second Caretaker asks the First: "Who is this girl that never comes? A sort of princess?" And the First answers: "Do you think that she exists?"

III

It is neither monastery, college nor castle, though in the course of centuries it may have been one or all of these. At one time it may even have been a prison. An establishment? That's the very word. A stopover for travelers? You could call it that. We were expecting you. This is the house to which people usually come.

So says Brother Tarabas to Jean. Jean, for his part, is very grateful. He's seen so many things, had so many adventures. All very interesting, but in the end exhausting. "And the journey's not over yet. I just need a little rest before I set out again." Rest he shall have, and food and drink ("I eat and drink, I eat and drink. And I'm still hungry, I'm still thirsty"). In return, he will relate all that he has seen and heard. The brothers gather to hear, even Brother Superior, all "looking like monks without quite looking like monks."

What have I seen? What have I seen? Oh, I've seen such a variety of things that I find it difficult to remember. Everything gets mixed up. Wait . . . Wait . . . I've seen people, I've seen meadows, I've seen houses, I've seen people, I've seen people, I've seen meadows. . . . Oh, yes . . . meadows and streams and rails . . . and trees. . . . (III,129)

He goes on and on in this vein, eating and drinking, listing noun after noun, juxtaposing mustaches and mountains, never qualifying, never elaborating, continually repeating himself. The brothers complain. But in the end Brother Tarabas, taking his cue from Brother Superior (who never says a word), tells Jean he found the talk—"or lecture, rather"—very precise and nicely textured.

As you must have noticed, our brothers were taking notes. . . . Nothing will be lost, not a word of what you've said. We are very grateful. Now we want you to relax and enjoy yourself. What would you say if we proposed a little show? . . . I hope it will be entertaining, and perhaps even educational. *Utile cum dulci* . . . (III,136)

There follows, as Bonnefoy observes, "a kind of parody of didactic theatre."[7] Jean is installed upon an elevated chair, and the brothers gather on either side of him, one side dressed in red, the other in black. The two main characters, Tripp and Brechtoll, who are acted by two of the brothers who used to be professional clowns, are brought out in cages. The sympathies of the brothers in black are with Tripp, those of the brothers in red with Brechtoll. Jean, however, expresses the anguish of both prisoners; he "participates," he identifies with both.

Brother Tarabas informs Jean that the play is about education and re-education. Tripp believes in God. He must be re-educated. Brechtoll does not believe in God. He must be re-educated. When Brechtoll says he believes in God, he will get his soup. When Tripp says he does not believe in God, he will get his soup. After forty minutes of actual playing time, Brechtoll turns theist and Tripp atheist, and they each get their soup.

What are we to make of this play within a play, given such emphasis both by length and position? Gabriel Marcel writes: "Everything permits us to suppose that the author wished to stigmatize the Inquisition under its religious form and its Communist form."[8] The author has his own comment: "There is also the fact that all the convictions for which we do battle are equivalent, that each one of us, if put in another situation, can believe the contrary of what he believed. There is a sort of levelling of values, or a nihilism."[9]

Ionesco possesses the kind of mind that, in the space of three pages, can set forth views about life and death and not call them, in any sense, an ideology and can reduce religion, in every sense, to ideology and praise a man like Pasternak for his convictions (as he does in *Notes and Counter Notes*) without recognizing their religious impulse. And then, in the interview quoted above, he can say that all convictions are equivalent and equate this with what a man can be made to say when placed in an extreme situation.[10]

But what has all this to do with Jean's search for happiness? That is precisely the point. In his comments, Ionesco talks about the play within the play quite apart from what it has to do with his main theme. The reason may well be that the connection isn't really there, that it is never *dramatically* established. It is possible, of course, to make a few guesses about what the connection is. Perhaps Jean is meant to see that happiness is to be found neither in religion nor in ideology, that they are one and the same thing, equally bad, equally irrelevant to the meaning of man. So he should stop looking. If that is the case, he has learned nothing, for after the show he says: "I must be on my way. To see what I haven't yet seen."

Or maybe the lesson he is supposed to learn is that in the attempt to experience everything (in the way that an ideology attempts to explain everything), one experiences nothing; in reaching for every value (in the way that an ideology lays claim to every value), one levels them all and ends up embracing a kind of nihilism. Jean does seem to sense this, though he does not connect it with the "educational theatre" to which he has been exposed. Like the Stranger in *Till Damaskus,* he bites into the "golden fruit" only to find it rotten inside:

> Everything I longed for would vanish at my approach, everything I tried to touch would wither. As soon as I made my way into a sun-drenched meadow, clouds would cover the sky. I was never able to take delight in anything. The grass dried up beneath my feet, the leaves on the trees turned yellow and fell to the ground as soon as I looked at them. If I tried to drink from the clearest spring, the water would become polluted, foul.
>
> (III,165)

Or perhaps Gabriel Marcel is right when he says that the entire third episode is situated "on the level of the gasp and the inarticulate."[11] And we should leave it at that.

At the end of the episode, Ionesco brings us clearly back to the main theme. Jean feels himself bound to tell the brothers everything, and he proceeds to describe the two fundamental states of his being: high elation, when the days were luminous and the universe was a source of wonder and delight and he felt no hunger, no thirst—or rather, when "this joy was his bread and water"—and deep depression, when the whole world seemed to fall into a pit, everything grew dark and hostile and hunger and thirst gnawed at his vitals, and this state was far more predominant. Why? What was expected of him? To suffer this hunger and thirst, to resign himself to it, to wait, to expect nothing, or to go in search of fulfillment?[12]

Jean feels he must continue on his search. "Tell me, brothers, what I owe you. I'm in a big hurry." But he has no money. He must render them "a little service" and then he will be free to go. At that moment, through the bars of the great gate, the garden of the first episode becomes visible to him, with blue sky and trees in bloom and the same silver ladder, and everything drenched with light. Marie calls to him; like Solveig for Peer Gynt, she has waited for him all this time. Their daughter Marthe is with her, by now a young girl of fifteen. "My darlings, oh my darlings!" Jean cries. "I thought I would never see you again. How happy I am now!" Now, it seems, he understands. Now he is frantic to discharge his debt. Brother Tarabas tells him what he must do:

> All we ask is that you serve a meal to these brothers sitting around the table, these brothers who look like wretched tramps, not because they haven't been fed, but because they are always famished, like you. You know how it is. When you have finished serving table, you can go and rejoin your family. . . .
> (III,169)

How long, how long will it take? The Brother Accountant begins counting the hours and they all take up the count. The figures begin multiplying on blackboards and walls as Jean hands out bowls and spoons and ladles out soup, over and over again.

La Soif et la faim, says Ionesco, "is the story of a wandering [*errance*], of a mistake [*erreur*] and its punishment."[13]

"We'll wait, we'll wait," Marie assures her husband. "I'll wait for you for as long a time as it takes, I'll wait for you forever."[14]

IV

"Theatre should not be an illustration of something already given. On the contrary, it is exploration."[15] Ionesco said this shortly after the Paris production of *Hunger and Thirst,* and one might well ask whether his play is not more illustration than exploration. The feeling persists, after several readings and one viewing,[16] that the play calls up echoes from *Peer Gynt, Waiting for Godot* and *Till Damaskus* without ever really finding a voice of its own. Part of the problem is its form, or lack of individuating form. One reviewer of the Paris production has written that "the performance of the Comédie's Robert Hirsch—now its bravura star—as Jean is what makes this strange, obscure play comprehensible. . . . It is so peculiar and fascinating a play that it demands Hirsch's brilliant, synthesizing performance to seem united."[17] Marcel will not even grant that. "What is missing, *c'est le souffle*. This play can yield no meaning except in a picaresque register; but this supposes a continuity that it never achieves."[18] It was probably this lack of continuity that prompted the English translator, Donald Watson, to insert, in the last scene of the third episode, several references to "the other one," the ideal woman of the second episode. Jean is made to shout to his wife: "And make her wait, too!" But these insertions are fatal: They say, in effect, that Jean has understood nothing.[19]

I have said that *Hunger and Thirst* is more illustration than exploration. But to the extent that the play *does* explore, it opens up an important aspect of pilgrimage. Gustave Thibon expresses this aspect admirably, if, for purposes of the play, we let the word *God* stand for whatever answers man's hunger and thirst:

> You feel you are hedged in; you dream of escape; but beware of mirages. Do not run or fly away in order to get free: rather dig in the narrow place which has been given you; you will find God there and everything. God does not float on your horizon, he sleeps in your substance. Vanity runs, love digs. If you fly away from yourself, your prison will run with you and will close in because of the wind of your flight; if you go deep down into yourself it will disappear in paradise.[20]

In *The Cocktail Party,* Celia and Edward and Lavinia find the narrow place that has been given them and the assumption is that they "will find God there and everything." Jean, in running away, locks himself in his own prison. He knows now how he got into it, and that is his special pain. Whether, like Kilroy in *Camino Real,* he can find a way out of his hell, we do not know. But the vision of Marie in the garden is always before him.

NOTES

[1] C.C., "Ionesco et Les Subventions," *Les Nouvelles littéraires* (February 24, 1966), p. 13.

[2] Ionesco has said that there are many dreams in *La Soif et la faim:* "the dream of the woman in the flames, the dream of someone in my family, someone dead, whom I see again dressed in a

bizarre fashion. I know in the dream that she is dead and it astonishes me to see her paying me a visit. And the dream of the cellar in the first act is a dream which I have fairly often: the dream of the sinking house. It is, in some sense, the tomb. Very often, in this dream, my mother appears. For the psychologist that might be rather significant" (Claude Bonnefoy, *Entretiens avec Eugène Ionesco* [Paris: Éditions Pierre Belfond, 1966], pp. 85f.).

[3] Eugène Ionesco, *La Soif et la faim,* in *Théâtre,* vol. 4 (Éditions Gallimard, 1966), p. 94. All references are to this edition, and all translations are my own.

[4] Heinrich Zimmer, as quoted in Eliade, *Myths, Dreams and Mysteries,* pp. 244f.

In Ionesco's play, after Aunt Adelaide's visit, a fireplace appears briefly in the back wall, and it is behind that wall that the garden appears. I would not be at all surprised to learn that Ionesco was familiar with the passage quoted above and that it was somehow operative when he began the play. At any rate, he counts Eliade among his friends, and in Bonnefoy's interview with him, cited above, there is reference to Eliade in connection with "archetypical dreams" (p. 38).

[5] Gabriel Marcel, *Homo Viator,* p. 34.

[6] See Marcel, p. 46: ". . . in so far as I make my hope conditional I myself put up limits to the process by which I could triumph over all successive disappointments."

[7] *Entretiens avec Eugène Ionesco,* p. 173.

[8] Gabriel Marcel, "Une Mesure pour rien," review of *La Soif et la faim, Les Nouvelles littéraires* (March 10, 1966), p. 13.

[9] *Entretiens avec Eugène Ionesco,* pp. 173f.

[10] In a later interview, conducted by Rosette Lamont and published after the completion of this chapter, Ionesco has this to say about the play within the play: "I wanted to portray people who hold a false faith, people such as Brecht, Lucien Goldmann, Kenneth Tynan. These extremists can easily change from one extreme to the opposite extreme. A man with an ideology has a greater tendency to espouse the opposite ideology than a man who has ideals." At the end of the same interview, when asked if he would have chosen to live in some century other than the twentieth, he replied that he would have so chosen: "A Biblical epoch" (*Massachusetts Review* X [Winter, 1969]: 119–27).

[11] Marcel, "Une Mesure pour rien," p. 13.

[12] A footnote in the Gallimard edition of the play indicates that this monologue was omitted in the Paris production. The two fun-

damental states that it describes are, in fact, dramatized in the second episode. Ionesco has said that all his plays "have their origin in two fundamental states of consciousness: now the one, now the other is predominant, and sometimes they are combined," and he proceeds to describe them at length (*Notes and Counter Notes,* pp. 35–37).

[13] *Les Nouvelles littéraires* (February 24, 1966), p. 13.

[14] In most of Ionesco's plays, woman is "a companion of darkness," as French critic Jean Mambrino, S.J., once described her. She appears in a somewhat different light in the later plays. Marie, in *Exit the King,* makes much of her love for the King, but in the end "this love is an illusion." On the other hand, something can be said for Marguerite as "the King's better half" (see Daniel Berrigan, S.J., "*Exit the King* and Crisis of America," *The Critic,* February-March, 1969: 21–25. Berrigan confuses the names of the two women). Marthe, in *A Stroll in the Air,* voices the faint hope that the fire will die and the ice melt, "and the gardens . . . the gardens . . ." But she is the hero's daughter, not his wife and companion. (See Guicharnaud, *Modern French Theatre,* rev. ed., p. 224, who puts down Marthe's hope as "an expression of Ionesco's wishful thinking.") Now, in *Hunger and Thirst,* Marie-Madeleine appears in the garden, promising to wait "for as long a time as it takes."

[15] *Entretiens,* p. 168.

[16] A production billed as the "English-speaking world premiere" by the Yale Dramat, an undergraduate organization, directed by Leland Starnes, in New Haven, Conn., 1967.

[17] Genêt (pen name for Janet Flanner), "Letter from Paris," *The New Yorker* (July 16, 1966), p. 101.

[18] "Une Mesure pour rien," p. 13.

[19] *Hunger and Thirst and Other Plays* (New York: Grove Press, 1969). Since the writing of this chapter, I have had the pleasure of seeing a second production of *Hunger and Thirst,* directed by Arthur Storch for the Berkshire Theatre Festival, 1969. Two developments give this production a special importance: Ionesco himself came to Stockbridge, Mass., for the rehearsals, and he has written an entirely new episode, "The Foot of the Wall," to replace "The Rendezvous." In this new episode there is no mention of the ideal woman, and instead of the terrace hanging in mid-air, there is an ancient wall, carved with history, dominating the scene. Jean has very little to say in this scene. He observes: a solicitous old couple, a callous young man and the twin sisters he toys with, a rabbi who later becomes a tourist guide, a judge and a convict. He

wants to pass through the wall, but he is warned against the attempt. The young man says flippantly: "Walls shelter us from the unknown, from chaos." Finally, the former rabbi, who is also something of a magician (with an air of evil about him, for he marched his children off the edge of a cliff), causes the wall to open for him. There Jean sees an old woman standing by a stove (see note 4). Ionesco has Jean refer to the old woman in the third episode, as having appeared to him several times. She points the way for him, even as she warns him against it. But off he goes. The new episode provides more entertainment and better continuity, but Jean is so detached from all that goes on around him that one may well question the dramatic necessity of this episode in terms of the total design, such as it is.

20 Quoted in *Homo Viator,* p. 28.

VIII. THE FUGITIVE

I

Ugo Betti reminded one of his critics that all of his heroes are "seekers after God," and "to seek after God," he wrote, paraphrasing Pascal, "means to have found Him."[1] Actually, in his last play, *The Fugitive,* he dramatizes a prior movement of the spirit: To flee from God means to seek Him. Or as he says in the funeral chant that ends the play:

> Even when we fled from You,
> We were on our way to You.

The flight from God *is* the journey toward Him.

The fugitive of the title is a young woman named Nina, wife of Daniele Manniscoli, a Deputy Registrar in a Northern Italian town. The first words are spoken by an "ironic and hostile" voice that Nina has heard many times before:

> What are you doing, Nina? Where are you going? *(Silence.)* Where will you go? Where will you flee? What will you do? *(Silence.)* Nina. Nina.[2]

But Daniele is also a fugitive, not only by complicity in Nina's crime, but also by his solidarity with her in her spiritual flight, and it is through him that Betti traces the path of that flight. Nina keeps asking *why,* but Daniele makes the question his own, and it is he who makes the thunder speak. Of such characters, Betti has said:

> The first exigency for a spirit which truly feels compassion and solidarity (and which is thirsting for the absolute) can only be this: to ask himself *why* he necessarily feels, mysteriously feels, such compassion, such solidarity. This question represents another, immediate step forward along the long path modern man will have to travel to find God again. It is this path I obstinately try to blaze.[3]

Through Daniele, then, we shall try to follow the path of the fugitive, the "underlying movement of spirit" which constitutes the action of the play.[4] This movement is nothing less than what has been described by Alfred North Whitehead as religion itself: "the passage from God the Void to God the Enemy and from Him to God the Companion."[5]

II

Daniele broods over God the Void in a mountain resort near the frontier. There is only one other guest, a mysterious "doctor of chemistry" who appears to be both priest and devil. When Daniele first meets him, he assumes the role of priest. "Do you believe in God?" he asks. And Daniele gives the same answer, in almost the same words, that Ysé gave in *Partage de Midi:* "I've never asked myself that question."

DOCTOR: And yet . . .
DANIELE: *(with a sweeping gesture)* I would like to find the meaning of it all. But I cannot.
DOCTOR: *(lightly)* Have you committed some crime?
DANIELE: No.
DOCTOR: Still you want to flee the country.

DANIELE: What gave you that idea?
DOCTOR: One comes here only for that.
DANIELE: As a matter of fact, I do have my troubles. And I'd like very much to put them behind me. (I,1487)

Before the conversation is over, Daniele has confessed that there were at least five reasons for running away: He got into numerous arguments with his boss, he embezzled a certain amount of money and incurred a number of debts, he wasn't getting on well with his wife, he was bored with provincial life and, last but not least, he knew that his wife was having an affair with his boss. The affair has its comic side: Nina has bought some rat poison. But there are no rats in the house.

The poison is not necessarily meant for Daniele. During the course of a card game, Nina's affair with Giulio, the Chief Magistrate, takes on implications that frighten them both. They have always played for money and Nina is greatly in debt, so this time she recklessly bets everything she owes him, double or nothing. What if she loses? Then, says Giulio, calling her his little garden, "I shall eat your juicy peaches, I shall bite the sweet rose, I shall taste your forbidden delights." She begs him to tear up "those little bits of paper," but Giulio refuses, hating himself all the while.

The card game, on one side of the stage, is played out against Daniele's conversation with the Doctor on the other side. When Nina and Giulio speak, Daniele and the Doctor freeze in place. Sometimes, the dialogue moves in counterpoint. When the Doctor urges Daniele to disengage himself, to "fly like the angels" across the mountains, Giulio is heard to say to Nina, "Lose again, sink down to the depths."

The Doctor urges Daniele to disengage himself because nothing, no one, is worth the trouble. Why does

Daniele exist? What brought him and his wife together? Pure coincidence. Chance. There is only the void. "Would you, by any chance, be the devil?" Daniele asks with a smile. Daniele, in flight from Nina, is drawn back to her. The Doctor asserts that his motive is revenge. Daniele is forced to admit it. Nina is responsible and must be punished. Why does she do what she does? Why does she hate me? Why?

Since Daniele is not satisfied with "the hypothesis of pure coincidence," the Doctor mockingly proposes another one: "motivated causes and clear-cut responsibilities," everything recorded either on the good side of the ledger or the bad side and then submitted to the Great Accountant. To the roll of thunder, the Doctor assumes the role of God. He imagines himself on the shore, "casting his net over the void" and bringing in a number of squalid fish, "pale fibers of the void." He picks up one of them and says, "You shall be called Nina." *(Nina, on the other side of the stage, rises from her card game, bewildered, agitated.)* "You had nothing and you are nothing. So that now, for everything you have, for everything you are, you are in my debt . . . *(savagely)* and I say you are *responsible!*" Then, echoing that voice, ironic and hostile, which thundered at the beginning of the play, he adds: "Where will you go? What will you do? Nina. Nina. How will you pay? That eye, always upon you. Those footsteps, always dogging you . . ." *(Nina lets out a muffled scream.)*

In anguish, Daniele protests that the Doctor's second hypothesis is as unacceptable as his first. In any case, he is returning home to Nina. To punish her, yes. But he realizes that there is another reason why, in his flight, he is drawn back to her: "I thought I heard her crying out. A cry . . . of great fear. A cry . . . that I've heard her utter before."

Void crying out to void.

III

After the card game, Giulio lords it over Nina: "There was a time when I did not exist for you. Now do you see me? Do I exist?" (I,1494). Giulio exists for her now because now she has put herself in his power. A nonentity before, he rises out of the void to confront her as an enemy. How shall she escape him? She again chooses to gamble: She poisons him.

What she does, in effect, is to challenge the Void: Either you do not exist for me, she says, in spite of that voice and those footsteps, or you shall exist as my enemy. I shall put myself in your debt, in your power. I shall commit a crime.

When Daniele returns home, Nina has already dragged Giulio's body into the bushes. She killed him, she says, because he told her that she would never have finished paying him. "Throw him in the lake," she pleads. Daniele obliges her, even though he sees (as we learn later) that Giulio is still alive. Under interrogation, Nina points to her husband and says to the Inspector: "He is to blame. For everything." Later, when the Doctor appears and questions Daniele about his wife's accusation, he excuses her: "It was her way of showing she had confidence in me." When the Doctor expresses bafflement, Daniele answers:

> Do you know what Nina reminds me of? *(Shrugs his shoulders.)* A rabbit. Yes. A rabbit that I saw some years ago. There it was, all bloody, in the trap. For a few moments it struggled madly. Then it lay still again, its eyes dilated, its sides working like a bellows. In struggling to free itself, it struck out at the hunter, digging its nails in his flesh. He, then, flung it to the ground, like this, and killed it. *(Reflects; shrugs his shoulders.)* I was for the rabbit. (II,1513)

For Daniele, too, the footsteps that follow after Nina belong now to God the Enemy. Later on, he will say to God the Companion: "You were our adversary, and we were yours, and we stood up to your face" (III,1535).

The Doctor has no use for Daniele's compassion. But Daniele tells him how he heard Nina's scream again. He wanted to run away, but instead he held her close, held her until, as the Doctor puts it, "the instrument gave up its sound."

DANIELE: It was as if the black wall of the world had split open, a blinding crack. Forgive me, I'm dramatizing. It was, I don't know, something that reached to the farthest shore . . . overflowed: beyond. The beyond of everything. There was . . . a kind of echo. . . .
DOCTOR: *(in a low voice)* Which expressed?
DANIELE: I don't know. Pain. But also . . .
DOCTOR: But also . . . ?
DANIELE: There was . . . a fierce . . . majesty, which made the hair stand on end . . . a calling to account in the presence of . . .
DOCTOR: *(with a muffled cry)* Of what?
DANIELE: *(his head slightly bent)* It's ridiculous to say it—but the next day, seeing her, I felt . . . a kind of respect. And astonishment. That those wide-open eyes of hers had been able . . . to look upon . . .
DOCTOR: *(vehement again)* Upon what?
DANIELE: *(as if in secret)* In short, it seemed to me that all this presupposed . . .
DOCTOR: Something abnormal?
(A silence.)
DANIELE: *(with a kind of gravity)* Something important.
(II,1518)

Daniele cannot tell the Doctor why a mere shriek should carry such importance. But what he does next expresses his conviction. When Giulio's body is dragged up from the lake, Daniele escapes with Nina in a car. Shots are fired. Nina is wounded.

But as in *Till Damaskus,* the "mysterious huntsman" follows after.

IV

Nina has gambled with her very life, her very heart and soul, and Daniele with her. To whom is the debt owed?

They hide high in the mountains, but one by one their creditors come. The Inspector comes and calls them to justice: "Being judged begins with being understood." Daniele scorns his justice. "It was justice that fired those shots at her. Drops of her blood have streaked the mountains. And the hunt goes on. What is she, then: a woman, or a rabbit?" (III,1524). But the Inspector says that it is not to him that their debt is owed. Before he goes off in the darkness, he points to an approaching townsman: "It's to him. The common man. The world." But the townsman doesn't want to meddle. "As far as I'm concerned, consider yourselves absolved. . . . It's no concern of mine." He points to another visitor. "That woman there. Settle your accounts with her." The woman is Signora Paola, mother of the murdered man. But she tells Daniele that if either he or Nina owes anything, they don't owe it to her, they owe it to Giulio: He is their creditor. But even Giulio absolves them. When he looked into Nina's eyes after drinking the poison, and she into his, he saw that her eyes, too, were filled with terror. "She confided something to me, and I to her, without speaking. We saw ourselves! Pleading, the both of us! And I experienced, for her and for me . . . the same anguish." Giulio's voice trails off in the darkness: "Your debt . . ." Another voice, edged with irony, finishes: ". . . is not owed to me."

It is the Doctor. "I know what you're thinking," he

says to Daniele. "Those obstinate footsteps that have followed you all the way up here—to whom do they belong? Who is it compelling you to flee even from here?" The Doctor insists upon settling the dispute that has arisen between them. "I hold a few good cards. I accept bets. Before dawn you will be mine." He goes right to the heart of the matter: "What do you see in that woman?" Important? Neither she nor anyone else is worth the trouble. All her sufferings are nothing more than sand stirred up by the wind. Daniele is not that wind. The sand has lashed him too. Why, then, does he insist upon listening for those footsteps behind him as if they belonged to someone who listened, someone whom the mountains will not stop?

At this point a new character enters the lists, *un nuovo interlocutore:* thunder, reverberating through the mountains, speaking that "immense language" which rumbled in Claudel's "stellar kettle" (III,1531).

Name him, the Doctor taunts, "your one true creditor," and he pretends to interpret the thunder: "Cain, Cain, where fliest thou? What hast thou done?" In Betti's short story *Caino,* the fugitive cries out: "Christ, I say to you that you are unjust!"[6] This is the cry that Daniele hurls at the thunder: *Non è giusto!* "There is no justice!" The mountains magnify the debate, the Doctor mocking, Daniele demanding, the thunder never changing. Finally, "his revolt turning into awe," Daniele cries out: "Why do you deny us everything? Why do you torment us, why do you exact so much from us? What is it you want?" Like Lear, he feels himself more sinned against than sinning. Nina, who has said nothing, hides her head in her hands.

In his *Book of Pilgrimage,* Rilke writes:

> Thou carest nothing for him who questions.
> With a gentle countenance
> Thou lookest upon those who bear burdens.[7]

Job also asked questions. But God's answer is addressed not so much to Job's questions as to his burdens. God has no use for religious rationalism, for the absolutizing of the need to know. William Lynch elaborates:

> God wishes to get below and above all the categories of our understanding. He does this, not by crushing man but by purifying all the categories and powers of the pure understanding. Thus the Book of Job is an appeal, not for an irrational theology or for placing God beyond reason (for that is not the question under discussion); rather it is an appeal for recognizing a personal relationship between God and man that is not satisfied by the statements of reason and justice. Justice is a noble form of reason, but it is not enough to explain the mysteries of suffering.[8]

If at this point of the play we will not be satisfied except by statements of reason and justice, then we will not be satisfied by Daniele's attempt to answer Nina's question: "Why did I cry out?"

> Those cries of yours! They were too much for us, they passed beyond us, they required an interlocutor! And they found one! Why would you have cried out like that, if there were not someone to hear? It was a dialogue. Oh yes, believe it, Nina. There was someone. (III,1535)

Then, facing the mountain from which the thunder sounds, he says what Mesa said to the stellar kettle: "It was you." From God the Void to God the Enemy and from Him to God the Companion.

The first lines of Nina's funeral chant express the belief that just as the grain of wheat presupposes the earth, man presupposes God. In almost the same words, Betti makes this belief his own in an essay entitled "Religion and the Theatre," which he wrote the same year as the play, the year of his death, 1953. He ends that essay by declaring that there is in every man, even the most unjust, "an 'unwarranted' need for mercy, for harmony, for solidarity, for immortality, for trust, for forgiveness, and, above all, for love."

> Christ waits for us there. A mercy and a love far greater than those pale imitations that the world has to offer. Here is a thirst for which the fountains of the earth are but ungenerous trickles. Each of these mysterious needs is the side of a perimeter, whose complete design, when we finally catch a glimpse of it, has one name: GOD.[9]

Jean, in *Hunger and Thirst,* runs away from himself and finds his prison everywhere. Daniele and Nina, in their hunger and thirst, flee from God and find that God is everywhere.

NOTES

[1] "Essays, Correspondence, Notes," trans. William Meriwether and Gino Rizzo, *TDR* VIII, No. 3 (Spring, 1964): 71.

[2] *La Fuggitiva,* A Drama in Three Acts, in *Teatro completo,* by Ugo Betti (Bologna: Cappelli, 1957), p. 1477. All references are to this edition, and all translations are my own.

[3] "Essays, Correspondence, Notes," p. 70.

[4] For further explanation of *action* as the "underlying movement of the spirit," see *Dante's Drama of the Mind* by Francis Fergusson, p. 92, quoted in Chapter I, note 22.

[5] Quoted in *Eclipse of God,* by Martin Buber (New York: Harper & Brothers, 1952), p. 51.

[6] *Raccolta di novelle* (Bologna: Cappelli, 1963), p. 56. This story first appeared in 1928.

[7] Quoted in *Homo Viator* by Gabriel Marcel (New York: Harper Torchbooks, 1962), trans. Emma Craufurd, p. 231.

[8] *Images of Hope* (New York: Mentor-Omega Books, 1966), p. 95.

[9] *Religione e Teatro,* with a dedication by Andreina Betti

(Brescia: Morcelliana, 1957), p. 33. My translation. The English translation published in *TDR* V, No. 2 (December, 1960) and reprinted in *Masterpieces of the Modern Italian Theatre,* ed. Robert W. Corrigan (New York: Collier Books, 1967) omits the word *"ingiustificato"* ("unwarranted") and the sentence *"Cristo ci attende là* ("Christ waits for us there").

IX. MY KINSMAN, MAJOR MOLINEUX

I

America is all things new. She is New England and New York and New Jersey. She is the New World, described by Puritan Edward Johnson as "the place where the Lord will create a new Heaven, and a new Earth in, new Churches, and a new Common-wealth together."[1] The eyes of all peoples will be upon her, the New City set upon a hill, the New Jerusalem destined to justify God's ways to man, not, like Milton, in the agony of Paradise Lost but in the ecstasy of Paradise Regained. Who would think that the spirit of Milton's Lucifer would ever become her spirit?

"I always think," says Robert Lowell, "that there are two great symbolic figures that stand behind American ambition and culture. One is Milton's Lucifer and the other is Captain Ahab: these two sublime ambitions that are doomed and ready, for their idealism, to face any amount of violence."[2]

Milton's Lucifer, who creates evil in the attempt to possess all good, and Melville's Ahab, who, in the attempt to destroy evil, murders all good with it. In the absolute quality of their idealism, resolutely pursued, even to violence, "these two sublime ambitions" are one in spirit and it is this spirit that Lowell has embodied in his impressive trilogy, *The Old Glory*. Brought together under the unifying symbol of the flag, the three plays form, in Robert Brustein's words, "a dramatic history of the American character."[3]

In the first play, *Endecott and the Red Cross,* a military governor in colonial America is forced against his natural inclinations to kill and burn, egged on by the fanaticism of the Puritans and the pretensions of the Anglican Royalists. In the third play, *Benito Cereno,* the mystery of a Spanish captain's plight batters against the complacency of the American mind: Who is slave, and who is master? Who is guilty? The clearest answer that Delano, the American, can give is six pistol shots. The middle play, *My Kinsman, Major Molineux,* based on Hawthorne's short story of the same name, is in the form of a journey, and is, for that reason, the only one that will directly concern us here. Set at a crucial moment in the nation's history, the eve of the American Revolution, Robin's search for his kinsman sucks him into a nightmare world where "the inflammation of the popular mind" (Hawthorne's phrase) leads inexorably to blood. He moves from the light of high-minded innocence to the dark knowledge of good and evil, at which point he is forced to ask, as if for the first time, Where am I going?

II

The movement from light to dark is prefigured in the play of light and dark upon the stage. A space is carved in the darkness like the hollow of a dream, and Robin stands at its center. He is a young man barely eighteen; he carries a heavy oak-sapling cudgel, but the impulse to violence is given initially to Robin's brother, a boy of ten or twelve.[4] The ferryman who carries Robin and his brother across the river is huge and has a white curling beard, and his dress, "although eighteenth century, half suggests that he is Charon." From the very start, then, it is half suggested that Robin's visit to the city is a dream-visit to a kind of hell. The dialogue carries the suggestion further:

> FERRYMAN: I'll take the crown for your return trip.
> *(Takes the coin.)*
> No one returns.
> ROBIN: No one?
> FERRYMAN: No one.
> Legs go round in circles here.
> This is the city of the dead.
> ROBIN: What's that?
> FERRYMAN: I said this city's Boston,
> No one begs here. Are you deaf?[5]

With our feet firmly planted on the soil of colonial America, we seem to feel the burning sands of another place, another time.

Robin asks the ferryman to direct him to his kinsman's mansion. The ferryman answers him in the voice of Charon:

> If you'll wait
> here, you'll meet him on his rounds.
> All our important people drift
> sooner or later to my ferry landing,
> and stand here begging for the moon.
> (67)

Then, reflecting suddenly the "inflammation of the popular mind," he holds up a boiled lobster, "the Major's spitting image." Two British redcoats march by. He calls them lobsterbacks, the Major's chicken lobsters: "You'll feel his grip behind their claws." But Robin is trusting: He likes the way they smiled.

At this point, reinforcing the dream atmosphere, Lowell's stage directions call for five miniature houses, lined across the stage and "in the style of a primitive New England sampler," to light up one by one and then go dark—a barber shop, a tavern, a white church, a shabby brick house with a glass bay window and a pillared mansion with the golden lion and the unicorn of England on its cornice. In brief coils of light we see the Barber, the Tavern Keeper, the Clergyman, the Prostitute and the Man with the Mask—all of whom Robin will meet in separate encounters.[6]

The Man with the Mask, later addressed as Colonel Greenough, is the most important figure for the events to follow. He wears a grayish mask covered with pocks and is dressed in a blue coat and white trousers like General Washington's. "His forehead juts out and divides in a double bulge. His nose is a yellow eagle's beak. His eyes flash like fire in a cave." When he comes out of the pillared mansion, which is Major Molineux's official residence, he says:

> My mind's on fire. This fire will burn
> the pocks and paleness from my face.
> Freedom has given me this palace.
> I'll go and mingle with the mob.
>
> (72)

Upon his departure the last house goes dark. Robin rubs his eyes in a daze, but proceeds, with his brother, in search of his kinsman, who swore that he would help Robin make his fortune and would teach the boy Latin. "We're in the dark," the Boy says, "and far from Deerfield." "We're in the city, little brother." Compared to the city, the country is a place of light.

The first man he meets, a representative of the colonial aristocracy, is the Man in Periwig. The two barbers appear and stand by as the first members of a gathering chorus. The seesaw attitude that the Man in Periwig takes toward Robin sets up a pattern for each subsequent encounter—a pattern that echoes the visual contrast between light and dark that has just played upon the scene. At first, he is open and friendly: "I'll be your guiding lamp in Boston" (74). But when Robin tells him whom he is looking for, the light goes out in the Man's voice: "Barber, this man's molesting me!" When the barbers close in, Robin's brother voices his refrain: "Brain him with your cudgel, Robin!" But Robin wisely backs off. "He isn't worth the Major's spit."

The next encounter occurs in the tavern. The Tavern Keeper's welcome, for all Robin knows, is lightsome: "I trust you'll stay; / nobody ever leaves this city" (77). For the benefit of the crowd, he teases Robin about his country origins. Robin, in his high-minded innocence, answers: "I'm on our village council. I've / read Plutarch." But when he adds that he has "connections," that his kinsman is Major Molineux, the mood of the crowd moves from light to dark. The Man with the Mask emerges from the midst of them, holding a silver Liberty Bowl aloft: "The Major dropped this lobster in / the bowl." And the boys are driven away, though the younger cries to Robin: "Stand and be a man!"

The light into which Robin now moves has the brash brightness of a woman's red skirt. She is men's "refuge from the church" (72) and their "refuge from despair" (82). She has been the Major's refuge, and will gladly make Robin happy: "A kinsman of the Major's is / my kinsman." But when the Watchman approaches, she slams the door on Robin and turns off her light. The Watchman curses the two boys—"Move, you filthy, sucking hayseed!"—and move they do, in spite of the younger boy's indignation: "Why don't you hit him, brother?"

The final encounter between light and dark, before the darkness has its way, is with the Clergyman. He comes carrying a large English flag on a staff, having just left the Major's house, of whom he says:

A good man—it's a pity though
he's so outspoken; other good men
misunderstand the Major's meaning.
He just handed me this British
flag to put above my pulpit—
a bit outspoken!

(90)

The Clergyman is about to lead Robin to his kinsman's house when the Man with the Mask bursts in, unrolling a Rattlesnake flag.

I have a present for you, Parson:
our Rattlesnake. "Don't tread on me!"
it says. I knew you'd want to have one.
Hang it up somewhere in church;
there's nothing like the Rattlesnake
for raising our declining faith.

(90–91)

Leaving Robin in the dark, the Clergyman hurries out with the two flags, waiting to see which one will billow with the wind.[7]

When the two boys, on their own, reach the pillared mansion where their kinsman lives, the Lion and Unicorn of England are gone and a large Rattlesnake flag is flying. Colonel Greenough, the omnipresent Man with the Mask, comes out of the house. Only half his face is mottled now, the other half is fiery red.[8] "I'm as healthy as the times," he says. "I am an image of this city." Lowell has Robin associate the Man with Hades, "city of the dead":

He is someone out of "Revelations"—
Hell revolting on its jailers.

(100)

When at last the Man's whole face turns red, the Clergyman finds his voice:

> How long, how long now, Men of Boston!
> You've faced the furious tyrant's trident,
> you've borne the blandishments of Sodom.
> The Day of Judgment is at hand,
> now we'll strip the scarlet whore,
> King George shall swim in scarlet blood,
> Now Nebuchadnezzar shall eat grass and die.
> How long! How long! O Men of Boston,
> behave like men, if you are men!
>
> (107)

In spite of himself, Robin is drawn into the gathering darkness. Earlier, when he had referred to his father, the Clergyman had said: "Call no man father." Major Molineux was also meant to be a father to him, helping him make his way in the world. Robin is beginning to learn something about fathers. As Lowell writes in his poem "Fall 1961":

> A father's no shield
> for his child.
> We are like a lot of wild
> spiders crying together,
> but without tears.[9]

Now the cry of the wild spiders becomes a shout. All around him, Robin hears the will of the people: "Down with Major Molineux!" And he sees Colonel Greenough. The pocks are no longer visible, his face seems all afire.

Into the midst of the crowd, in a red cart, comes Major Molineux, partly tarred and feathered, one cheek bleeding, his red British uniform torn. "Oh my kinsman, my dear kinsman," cries Robin, still unconsciously holding the Rattlesnake flag that the Clergyman had handed him when he rose to speak. Slowly the Major stretches out his right arm and points to him: "Et tu, Brute!" The ferryman appears and the Major pleads with him to save him. "There's no returning on my boat," the ferryman says, and hits him on the head with an oar. The Major screams, and lies still. "All tyrants must die as this man died." One by one, they proclaim it—the ferryman, the Clergyman, the Man in Periwig, the Tavern Keeper, the Prostitute—until the Man with the Mask, plunging his sword into the Major's body, cries out: "Sic semper tyrannis!"[10]

The crowd disperses. The Boy, who all along has been looking for a flintlock, finds one. "Well, that's all I came to Boston for, I guess. / Let's go, I see the ferryman." But Robin takes his brother's hand and turns "firmly" toward the city. Robin's decisive gesture must not be overlooked. His decisiveness is in marked contrast to the Boy's indifference, so that he cannot be said to be, at this moment, "without will or desire," as one critic, Baruch Hochman, has described his state of mind.[11] Those words would better describe Hawthorne's Robin, who admits to weariness and asks the way back to the ferry but stays on at another's suggestion. Lowell's Robin makes up his own mind and speaks it firmly:

> Yes, brother, we are staying here.
> Look, the lights are going out,
> the red sun's moving on the river.
> Where will it take us to? . . . It's strange
> to be here on our own—and free.
>
> (113)

The lights are going out, and Robin is filled with the dark knowledge of good and evil. He is free, but the roots of that freedom are bathed in blood.

III

"Legs go round in circles here," the ferryman had said. Must they do so forever? Is history nothing but a wheel forever turning, the "Grand Mechanism" that Jan Kott talks about in his critique of Shakespeare's Historics? Bolingbroke supplants Richard, the Lord's Anointed; after Bolingbroke comes the glory of Henry V. Then, on a tide of blood, Division and Disorder. Is history nothing but "a mechanism whose cogs are both great lords and hired assassins; a mechanism which forces people to violence, cruelty and treason; which constantly claims new victims"?[12]

In the Old Testament Book of Kings, we seem to see the same mechanism at work. David supplants Saul, the Lord's Anointed; after David comes the glory of Solomon. Then, on a tide of blood, Division and Disorder. But in the Book of Kings, the "Grand Mechanism" of history is in tension with what we might call the "Great Dynamic" of God's salvific will, a thing of faith and hope.[13] Where the Grand Mechanism makes of the historical process a great wheel of power, endlessly and absurdly revolving, the aim of the Great Dynamic is to turn the process into a pilgrimage through time, reaching its fulfillment in God. Do we find any such tension in *My Kinsman, Major Molineux?*

We find it in the use that is made of God's words. Subtly but unmistakably, the biblical strength of these words pulls against the perverted meaning they take on in the mouths of the speakers. At one point, the Man with the Mask says to Robin: "The last shall be first, my Boy." Robin asks: "What do you mean? You talk like Christ." Yes and no. Words that Christ spoke in relation to a kingdom not of this world are used to justify the Grand Mechanism: "The first shall be last, my Boy" (97). To the

Clergyman Robin declares: "My father says the Church is a rock." "Yes, yes," the Clergyman answers, "a rock is blind. That's why / I've shut my eyes" (101). Later, he says: "The Church gets more enlightened every day. / We've learned to disregard the Law / and look at persons" (105). A more devastating half-truth there never was. When he sees which way the wind is blowing, his perverting of God's word slips into blasphemy: "Wherever the spirit calls me, I must follow" (106). God's spirit becomes the wind of political expediency.

One of the Clergyman's statements is in open conflict with the Bible. "We have an everlasting city," he says (71), speaking within the same context of belief as the Clergyman of the first play in the trilogy: "Here in America, we are in Israel" (21). And like the Israelites, in the name of the Great Dynamic, "We must free our land of strangers, even if each mile is a marsh of blood!" (28). But this is nothing more than an expression of the primitive ban, or *herem,* by which the early Israelites justified the mass murders of hostile peoples. It is certainly not the teaching of the prophets, nor of the Christ whose coming they prophesied. By urging such teaching in the name of the Great Dynamic, the two clergymen of *The Old Glory* oil the Grand Mechanism with blood.

The knowledge of good and evil that came with Adam's Fall comes to Robin and the young America with the very Idea of Progress. As Roy Harvey Pearce observes, one myth meshes with the other to form the Original Sin. Lowell, like Hawthorne, "would do no less than define the sense in which all the good that descended from violence in the past was inextricably tied to the evil which the violence produced, so that insofar as one profited righteously from the good, one was guilty of the evil." According to this belief, "only through the discovery of historical responsibility (i.e., responsibility *for* history) could a man gain whatever of human freedom he might aspire to."[14]

"It's strange / to be here on our own—and free." But that freedom is ambivalent from the very start. The desire to possess all good cannot be expressed in the spirit of Lucifer. That spirit goes against the Great Dynamic. The desire to destroy all evil cannot be pursued in the spirit of Ahab. That spirit feeds into the Grand Mechanism.

Shortly before the Clergyman stands up to harangue the people, Robin looks into the empty church. "A single restless ray" of moonlight "has crept / across the open Bible" (100), as if to say: "God's word is here. You have not heard it. There is only one Spirit by which to possess good and destroy evil. You have not lived it."

Not just individuals, like Daniele and Nina in *The Fugitive,* but whole nations, because of their crimes, can be in flight from God. Can we say, with the apostle Paul, that such nations "feel their way" toward God (Acts 17:27)? The first step is surely recognition of what spirit it is that makes them criminal:

> the red sun's moving on the river.
> Where will it take us to?

NOTES

[1] Quoted in William A. Clebsch's *From Sacred to Profane America* (New York: Harper & Row, 1968), p. 44. See also Perry Miller's *Errand into the Wilderness* (Cambridge, Mass.: The Belknap Press of Harvard University Press, 1956).

[2] A. Alvarez, "A Talk with Robert Lowell," *Encounter* XXIV (February, 1965): 42.

[3] Introduction to *The Old Glory,* p. xi. Reprinted with the permission of Farrar, Straus & Giroux, Inc., from *The Old Glory* by Robert Lowell, copyright © 1964, 1965, 1968 by Robert Lowell.

4 The younger brother is not to be found in the short story. The creation of such a character is, of course, dramatically useful for bringing out feelings and information, but at the same time it makes Robin's nature seem more temperate.

5 *The Old Glory*, p. 66. *My Kinsman, Major Molineux* is the only one of the three plays that is written in verse, in four-beat, unrhymed lines. During an informal discussion at the Yale School of Drama, in April, 1967, Lowell said that the other two plays, written in prose, were put into the form of free verse at the request of his publisher.

6 The Clergyman does not appear in the short story. On the other hand, one of Hawthorne's characters is omitted in the play, the "gentleman" who befriends Robin and stands by as a detached observer of the action. A couple of the questions addressed to him by Robin are, in the play, addressed to the Clergyman.

7 The flags do not appear in Hawthorne's story, but one or more flags figure in each of the three plays, making visible the irony of the title, *The Old Glory*. Several early American flags used the rattlesnake design. Benjamin Franklin is credited with having suggested it. "The flag of the Virginia colony was white or yellow and had a coiled rattlesnake in the center and underneath the motto 'Don't Tread on Me.' The First Navy Jack of 1775 was striped alternately red and white. Across the stripes stretched a rattlesnake under which was the motto 'Don't Tread on Me.' The flag of the Culpepper Minute Men was white. It had a rattlesnake in the center—above, the words 'Liberty or Death,' below, the familiar slogan 'Don't Tread on Me' " (Cleveland H. Smith and Gertrude R. Taylor, *Flags of All Nations* [New York: Thomas Y. Crowell Co., 1946], p. 8).

8 Here is Hawthorne's description: "One side of the face blazed an intense red, while the other was black as midnight, the division line being in the broad bridge of the nose; and a mouth which seemed to extend from ear to ear was black or red, in contrast to the color of the cheek. The effect was as if two individual devils, a fiend of fire and a fiend of darkness, had united themselves to form this infernal image." Black never appears on the face of Lowell's Man. Having chosen to suggest the disease of the times by a mask of "pocks and paleness," Lowell leaves him with half his face mottled.

9 *For the Union Dead* (New York: Farrar, Straus and Giroux, 1965), p. 11.

10 In the short story, Robin's apparent involvement in the revolt is shown not by his holding the flag, but by his joining, in

spite of himself, in the "convulsive merriment" that greeted Major Molineux. "The contagion was spreading among the multitude, when, all at once, it seized upon Robin, and he sent forth a shout of laughter that echoed through the street; every man shook his sides, every man emptied his lungs, but Robin's shout was the loudest there." In the short story, the Major's end is not described: "When there was a momentary calm in that tempestuous sea of sound, the leader gave the sign, the procession resumed its march. On they went, like fiends that throng in mockery around some dead potentate, mighty no more, but majestic still in his agony. On they went, in counterfeited pomp, in senseless uproar, in frenzied merriment, trampling all on an old man's heart. On swept the tumult, and left a silent street behind."

[11] "Robert Lowell's *The Old Glory*," *TDR* XI (Summer, 1967): 129.

[12] *Shakespeare Our Contemporary* (Garden City, N.Y.: Doubleday Anchor Books, 1966), p. 38.

[13] This tension is also very much in evidence in Shakespeare's Histories. By rubbing it out, Kott displaces the mainspring of drama in these plays.

[14] "Hawthorne and the Sense of the Past, or, The Immortality of Major Molineux," *Journal of English Literary History* XXI (December, 1954): 334.

CONCLUSION

All theatre makes man pause, as it were, in his journey through time, but the Theatre of Pilgrimage makes him pause precisely in order to ask where he is going. And it leaves the future open.

This last element needs to be stressed. It is not enough to ask the question and then put out every light. I would like to have included Eugene O'Neill's *Long Day's Journey into Night* among the plays discussed, but in the end I had to agree with Tom F. Driver: "The long day's journey takes us . . . back into the past. Bulky, and 'real,' the past is so overpowering that the future is obliterated."[1] This is to say nothing about the quality of the play's achievement, only that it is not theatre of pilgrimage, as I have defined it.

The pull of the future is the one element in theatre of pilgrimage that would justify the consideration of a playwright whose name in this context might at first sound surprising: the Marxist Bertolt Brecht. His Marxism, of course, is the very thing that puts him in the Judaeo-Christian tradition, even if ambiguously. One of his plays, *The Exception and the Rule,* is "the story of a journey undertaken by one who exploits and two who are exploited."[2] The rule is cruelty and compassion the exception. The play itself dramatizes the rule, and at the end the actors address the audience: You have seen the abuse; now find the remedy. Change, in other words, is possible; the past is not decisive; the future is open. The leading theoretician of the French Communist Party, Roger Garaudy, feels that on this point Marxists and Christians can agree. Christian thinkers such as Teilhard de Chardin, he says, have posed "the basic problem of our century, the very problem that Marx posed for the first time a century ago and which he began to answer: how to think the law of change and how to master it."[3] That is something that Brecht's Mother Courage could never do, and that is her tragedy.

Negro spirituals are so filled with the theme of pilgrimage that I expected with some confidence to find that theme embodied in a play about blacks. Marc Connelly's *Green Pastures* might have qualified, but because its portrayal of the Negro is under suspicion today, I decided not to include it. A number of plays by black playwrights reflect the theme of pilgrimage in their very title—Frank Wilson's *Walk Together, Children;* Hall Johnson's *Run, Little Children;* Louis Peterson's *Take a Giant Step,* to mention a few[4]—but none of these seemed important enough for purposes of this study. The same must be said for Langston Hughes's *Tambourines to Glory,* in spite of its fine pilgrimage songs. James Baldwin's *Blues for Mister Charlie* ends with a freedom march in protest against the murder of a young black. The march might have provided the play with the framework it sorely needs; instead, the metaphorical dimension of pilgrimage is only slightly hinted at. The subway in LeRoi Jones's *Dutchman* is clearly metaphorical, doomed, like the phantom ship, to run its course forever: The only way for the black man to get off is to murder or be murdered. By its own lights, the play finds no way to move except in gear with the Grand Mechanism. It is not, therefore, in the last analysis, theatre of pilgrimage. I remain convinced, however, that the play which aspires to express, in its stride and scope, the spirit of the black people will have to be a pilgrimage play.

I have borrowed so much from Gabriel Marcel as a philosopher and critic that I regret having had to pass him by as a playwright. His theatre, which he has called "The Drama of the Soul in Exile," has even been referred to as "a theatre of pilgrimage," though not in the sense in which I have defined it.[5] *Ariadne (Le Chemin de Crète),* the play Marcel considers to be his most significant, qualifies as a pilgrimage play, but I did not feel that its metaphor of pilgrimage was operative enough to warrant inclusion of the work in this initial study.

There are, of course, still other pilgrimage plays that I might have considered, among them Ibsen's early poetic drama *Peer Gynt* and his last play, *When We Dead Awaken;* one of Strindberg's early plays, *Lucky Per's Journey,* and his last play, *The Great Highway;* Claudel's sprawling baroque drama *The Satin Slipper.* But I hope that from our excursions into the eight plays chosen for this study an idea of the Theatre of Pilgrimage has emerged.[6] "Where do we come from? What are we? Where are we going?" The Theatre of Pilgrimage, in asking these questions, leaves open the possibility of faith as a way of knowing *(King Lear).* The world it looks out upon is not opaque, but has the quality of sign, though the danger of illusion is always present *(The Road to Damascus).* The past is not seen as decisive: A man is still free to enter the future, destination unknown, with faith not only as a way of knowing but also as a way of loving *(The Cocktail Party).* Love transfigures even as it crucifies, if a man can say yes to the cross *(Break of Noon).* Even if he must descend into hell, he can still push toward resurrection *(Camino Real).* He does not have in himself his own fulfillment, but if he runs away from himself, riding on hopes too long or too short, he takes his prison with him *(Hunger and*

Thirst). If, indeed, he runs away from a God whose footsteps he has heard, he has already begun the journey toward Him *(The Fugitive).* His journey is not an isolated process, it is caught up in mankind's pilgrimage through history, in which the Grand Mechanism is in tension with the Great Dynamic *(My Kinsman, Major Molineux).*

The Theatre of Pilgrimage is a theatre in which man, in his going forward, would free himself of every illusion but will not close his mind to mystery.

NOTES

[1] "On the Late Plays of Eugene O'Neill," in *Man in the Modern Theatre,* ed. Nathan A. Scott, Jr. (Richmond, Va.: John Knox Press, 1965), p. 42.

[2] *The Jewish Wife and Other Short Plays,* English versions by Eric Bentley (New York: Grove Press, 1965), p. 111.

[3] "Communists and Christians in Dialogue," *New Theology No. 5,* ed. Martin E. Marty and Dean G. Peerman (New York: Macmillan Co., 1968), p. 221.

[4] See *Dark Symphony: Negro Literature in America,* ed. James A. Emanuel and Theodore L. Gross (New York: The Free Press, 1968), pp. 361–65.

[5] Richard Hayes, in his Introduction to Gabriel Marcel: *Three Plays* (New York: Hill & Wang, 1965). Hayes's definition: "journeys to the interior undertaken in a climate of magnetic silence charged with memory and affectivity" (p. 7).

[6] I like to speak, too, of a cinema of pilgrimage. Any film that depicts man in his search for meaning can be understood in terms of pilgrimage, but there are some excellent films in which a metaphor of pilgrimage is operative, not only among such classics as *La Strada, La Dolce Vita* or *The Seventh Seal,* but, significantly, also among more recent films, such as *2001: A Space Odyssey, Teorema, Midnight Cowboy, Easy Rider* and *The Milky Way.*

Appendix

Related Readings

Because hope is so much a part of pilgrimage, I have included these extracts in the hope that they will buttress the general ideas set forth in my introductory chapter and that more than one of them will illumine the movement of spirit embodied in a particular play. All extracts are reprinted by permission of the publishers.

Hope and History

Tom F. Driver, *The Sense of History in Greek and Shakespearean Drama*

In Hellas, the absence of a radical notion of creation went hand in hand with an understanding of time as essentially closed. The possibility of the new was excluded, for the reduction of time to the measure of change in a finite world meant that eventually all situations would recreate themselves.

In Israel, the conception of Yahweh's creativity meant an understanding of time as potentially open. As Yahweh in the beginning had created man, earth, heaven, and all the natural beings, so he had created the people Israel in their covenant relation with him, had created their law, made them a nation, and preserved them in adversity. All this implied a purpose which, obviously not fulfilled now, would be made perfect in the future. (New York & London: Columbia University Press, 1967, p. 49)

Walter Ong, S.J., "Evolution, Myth, and Poetic Vision"

For the Christian, both the universe and the life of the individual man end in quite different states from those in which they began. Time makes a difference. Time tells. Christian teaching urges no one to try to recover a lost Eden. Salvation lies ahead, at the end of time. And Adam's sin, which drove man from the Garden of Eden, is even hailed in the Holy Saturday liturgy of the Roman Catholic Church as *felix culpa,* "happy fault," because it gave God occasion to send His Son Jesus Christ to redeem man. The promise of the future is thus greater than that of the past. Christian (and Hebrew) teaching underlines the nonrepetitiveness of actuality and by the same token the importance of the unique, unrepeatable, human self, the human person. Christianity, like evolutionary thinking, is anticyclic. (*New Theology No. 5,* ed. Martin E. Marty and Dean G. Peerman [New York: Macmillan Co., 1968], pp. 244–45)

Rubem A. Alves, *A Theology of Human Hope*

The community of faith understood that it lived in a world of expanding horizons, always being made open to possibilities nonexistent before. Human life was thus seen as a happening in history, in a time which was open-ended in the direction of the future. . . . G. E. Wright observes: "We can never be certain of the true reason for this particular Israelite view of nature and history. It is the primary, irreducible datum of Biblical theology, without antecedents in the environment whence it might have evolved." This vocation of freedom stood in sharp opposition to all the then prevalent models of human life and society which were shaped according to the pattern of nature and cyclical time and which, consequently, understood human life in terms of adaptation to the given, natural structures of life. (Washington/Cleveland: Corpus Books, 1969, p. 76)

Johannes B. Metz, *Theology of the World.* Trans. William Glen-Doepel

Recent exegetical researches indicate that the words of Revelation in the Old Testament are not primarily words of statement or of information, nor are they mainly words of appeal or of personal self-communication by God, but they are *words of promise.* Their statement is announcement, their announcement is proclamation of what is to come, and therefore the abrogation of what is. . . . This dominant proclamation and word of promise initiates the future: it establishes the covenant as the solidarity of the Israelites who hope, and who thereby experience the world for the first time as a history which is oriented to the future. This Hebrew experience and thought stand in contrast to Greek thought, which understands the world not as a history oriented to the future, but as a closed cosmos or as a subsisting world of nature. This Hebrew thought is contained in those important passages of the Old Testament which are impregnated with a pathos for the new *(das Novum)*, for the new time and the new coming world, i.e., for the new as that which *never* was. Greek thought, in contrast to Hebrew thought, considers that which has never been as intrinsically impossible, since for the Greeks there is "nothing new under the sun." Everything which will come in the future is only a variation of the past and an actualization or confirmation of the *anamnesis.* History is therefore only the indifferent return of the same within the closed realm of the eternal cosmos. Since the essence of history is here considered as cyclic, history is seen as devouring her own children over and over again, so that there is nothing new in history, and the essence of history reveals itself as nihilistic. We emphasize this contrast between Hebrew and Greek understanding of the world in order to show that the biblical viewpoint considers the world as a *historical* world, in so far as it is a world "arising toward" God's promises under the responsibility of the Israelites, who hope in these promises. This understanding is reflected in the Genesis creation narratives, which were originally narratives of God's promises (so that they therefore express not merely a faith in a past creation, but a faith in the new creation of God's promises). The revelation of God's name in Exodus 3,14 also indicates that this eschatological horizon is the central aspect of God's revelation. The expression "I am who I am" is much better translated as "I will be who I will be." (So Gerhard von Rad and Martin Buber and a footnote in the RSV.) According to this version God revealed himself to Moses more as the power of the future than as a being dwelling beyond all history and experience. God is not "above us" but "before us." His transcendence reveals itself as our "absolute future." This future is grounded in itself, and is self-possessed. It is a future that is not erected out of the potentialities of our human freedom and human action. Rather, this future calls forth our potentialities to unfold themselves in history. Only such a future—one that is more than just the projections of our abilities—can call us to realize truly *new* possibilities, to become that which has *never* existed. "I will be who I will be." The future proclaimed here does not get its power from our present wishes and effort. No, its power stems from itself: it belongs to itself. Only thus can and does this future exert its stirring and liberating power over *every* human present, over *every* generation. (New York: Herder & Herder, 1969, pp. 87–89)

Rubem A. Alves, *A Theology of Human Hope*

In the historical experience of the community, the sabbath was a day of rest "on the way toward" a new tomorrow. It was a pause not in the routine of cyclical time but rather a moment of relaxation on the way toward a new day. . . . It was a pause in the movement toward the new. Its dehistorization, however, robbed it of this dimension, destroyed its character of pause in the expectation of the creation of the new. The time of the sabbath became similar to the cyclical time of the religions of nature: man had to adapt, to fit in, to be in harmony with, and to abdicate the creation of anything new. (p. 81)

Rubem A. Alves, *A Theology of Human Hope*

The historical time created by God's messianic activity is . . . radically opposed to organic time, the time of nature. In organic time the present receives the past, nay the present emerges from the past by repetition or evolution. The present is thus the presence of the past. Within historical time, however, the past that was about to determine the present is penetrated by freedom. Through this act the unfolding of the immanent possibilities of "what was" is interrupted and the new is inserted into the present. The present becomes thus a pregnancy in which a new future already determines the present toward a historical tomorrow. The future is therefore being engendered now, amid the history where man is living, compelling him to respond to the vectors of the events that are bearers of freedom. Hope is possible and real because now, in the center of history, new historical liberating events are being created. (pp. 96–97)

Carl E. Braaten, "Toward a Theology of Hope"

For Ernst Bloch the key to human existence is to be found in the hopes which man holds for the future state of humanity and the world. What fires man's spirit in the present is the radiation which emanates from "the promise of a 'transcendental' homeland where all who now suffer, labor, and are incomplete will find their true identity. In the 'radiation' from this utopian state, an attempt is made to discover the ultimate meaning of human existence. This radiation derives from an unshakable confidence that there will be a new life or *novum ultimum*" (Moltmann). Bloch, a Jewish-Marxist atheist, draws much of his understanding of man's directedness toward the future from the prophetic history of the Bible. He says, "Man is indebted to the Bible for his eschatological consciousness." As Moltmann puts it, Bloch accepts the "major objects of hope in the Bible" without belief in the transcendent personal God of Judaism and Christianity. It is a "hope without faith," or a "humanism without God." What is significant is that Bloch's view of man provides a point of contact for the biblical promise of the kingdom of God. Man as such is open-ended toward the future; this openness is evident in his hopes. Bloch makes the categories of possibility, of the new, of futurity, fundamental in his "ontology of not-yet-being." (*New Theology No. 5,* pp. 96–97)

Hope and Hopelessness

William F. Lynch, S.J., *Images of Hope*

There is nothing wrong with hopelessness as long as it does not get into our hope. What I mean is what G. K. Chesterton meant about wine when he said: "I don't care where the water goes if it doesn't get into the wine." (New York & Toronto: Mentor-Omega Books, 1966, p. 38)

William F. Lynch, S.J., *Images of Hope*

One of the best safeguards of our hopes, I have suggested, is to be able to mark off the areas of hopelessness and to acknowledge them, to face them directly, not with despair but with the creative intent of keeping them from polluting all the areas of possibility. (p. 51)

William F. Lynch, S.J., *Images of Hope*

If hope means a number of things, it certainly means the ability to wait. It means this by substance and by definition. For by definition it means that we wish a difficult future good or that we are in trouble and cannot yet see the way out. It means that we decide to wait.

The decision to wait is one of the great human acts. It includes, surely, the acceptance of darkness, sometimes in defiance. It includes enlarging one's perspective beyond a present moment, without quite seeing the reason for doing so. Fortitude and endurance are there, to an extent, beyond the merely rational. Waiting is sometimes an absolute, which chooses to wait without seeing a reason for waiting. It does not ignobly accept such pseudo-reasons as "don't worry," "don't fret," "don't be silly," "listen to better judgment," "a Christian knows there is no reason for stress." It simply chooses to wait, and in so doing it gives the future the only chance it has to emerge. It is, therefore, the most fundamental act, not the least act, of the imagination. (p. 152)

Sam Keen, "Hope in a Posthuman Era"

The question of God is not the question of the existence of some remote infinite being. It is the question of the possibility of hope. The affirmation of faith in God is the acknowledgment that there is a deathless source of power and meaning that can be trusted to nurture and preserve all created good. To deny that there is a God is functionally equivalent to denying that there is any ground for hope. It is therefore wholly consistent for Sartre to say that human beings "must act without hope," or for Camus to warn that hope was the last of the curses which Pandora took from her box. If God is dead, then death is indeed God, and perhaps the best motto for human life is what Dante once wrote over the entrance to hell: "Abandon hope, all ye who enter." (*New Theology No. 5,* pp. 86–87)

Erich Fromm, *You Shall Be as Gods*

The dynamic psalm [such as Psalm 22, "My God, my God, why hast thou forsaken me?"] shows the inner struggle within the poet to rid himself of despair and to arrive at hope. Thus we find that the movement takes on the following form: it starts in some despair, changes to some hope, then returns to deeper despair and reacts with more hope; eventually it arrives at the very deepest despair and only at this point is the despair really overcome. The mood has definitely changed, and in the following verses of the psalm there is no experience of despair, except as a receding memory. The psalm is the expression of a struggle, a movement, an active process occurring within a person; while in the one-mood psalm the poet wants to confirm an existing feeling, in the dynamic psalm his aim is to transform himself in the process of saying the psalm. The psalm is a document of the victory of hope over despair. It also documents an important fact: that only when the frightened, despairing person experiences the full depth of his despair can he "return," can he liberate himself from despair and achieve hope. As long as the full despair has not been experienced, he cannot really overcome it. He may overcome it for a while, only to fall back into it after a time. The cure of despair is not achieved by encouraging thoughts, not even by feeling *part* of the despair; it is achieved by the seeming paradox that despair *can be overcome only if it has been fully ex-*

perienced. (New York: Holt, Rinehart and Winston, 1966; Greenwich, Conn.: Fawcett Publications, 1969, pp. 163–64)

Hope and Experience

Gabriel Marcel, *Homo Viator.* Trans. Emma Craufurd

If we accept the perspective of established experience, we are led to suppose that time will bring nothing new beyond an illustration or an added confirmation, actually superfluous, of the pronouncements engraved on the tables of universal wisdom or merely common sense. It is as much as to say that we are here in a world where time no longer *passes,* or, which comes to the same thing, where time merely passes without bringing anything, empty of any material which could serve to establish a new truth or inspire a new being. (New York: Harper Torchbooks, 1962, p. 52)

Sam Keen, "Hope in a Posthuman Era"

It is important to realize that the believer is clear that experience renders an ambiguous verdict. In both the inner and the outer world it is as Ecclesiastes has told us: there is both building up and tearing down, creating and destroying. And if the life force seems ingenious in circumventing all that threatens life and growth, it is nevertheless true that finally death wins. Thus the question of hope becomes the question of the adequacy and the finality of the categories of human understanding. . . .

Although I have the greatest admiration for the heroic spirit of Camus, I do not think we should confuse the style of life he recommends with any form of religious or Christian faith. *He* did not. Religious faith involves a movement in which the believer goes beyond the categories of present experience and posits a meta-empirical ground for hope. This is precisely the movement Camus refused to make. He wished to live in the certainties and to live without appeal. To eliminate the movement beyond the certainties of the present moment of experience is not to make Christianity palatable to the empirical and secular mind of the 20th century. It is to eliminate the religious option. (*New Theology No. 5,* pp. 87–89)

Josef Pieper, *Hope and History*

What becomes of our hopes if we must die after all? Hope is directed towards salvation; but "salvation is nothing if it does not free us from death." This last sentence from the work of Gabriel Marcel seems to me entirely persuasive, whereas I do not understand a word of what Ernst Bloch has to say on this subject, namely that "the certainty of class consciousness . . . is a *novum* against death," a "remedy against death." To be sure, it is true that "the class" does not die, any more than does society or the cosmos or even "evolution." Only the individual person dies. But precisely here lies the ground for that link between death and hope which nothing can shatter. It is absurd to imagine that a collective (the *genus homo,* the universe, nature) is capable of hoping; in any case, to speak in such terms would be to misuse the word. Strictly speaking, hope, exactly like dying, can only be the act of a person. To say this is naturally not to count on the possibility that death can ever be eliminated from the world. And of course it is wrong to assert that it is senseless to hope as long as the hoper must physically die. (New York: Herder & Herder, 1969, pp. 70–71)

Hope and Technology

Rubem A. Alves, *A Theology of Human Hope*

Herbert Marcuse, in *One-Dimensional Man,* suggests that the signs and wonders that the language of technologism presents as the ground for the hope of liberation, instead of making possible the creation of a new future by a free man, do just the opposite. Marcuse points out that in the so-called technological society technology is no longer the tool which, in the hands of free man, is necessary for the creation of a better world. It has rather become a system which envelops, conditions, and determines man. It is, indeed, creating a new type of man who has become one-dimensional and fat through the goods that the technological system creates. Man no longer simply uses technology; he is now a part of the total technological system. Consequently he is made incapable of critical thinking and action, futureless and ahistorical, at home in a system that is now his home and his permanent tomorrow. (p. 22)

Rubem A. Alves, *A Theology of Human Hope*

When we discussed the results of colonialism on the colonial peoples we indicated that it was able to create an oppressed consciousness, that is, a consciousness which is domesticated and deprived of its futuricity. It did this by making the vision of the future impossible for the oppressed man. In the technological societies the same oppressed consciousness is again created but now for a different reason: because the future is no longer necessary. If the system gives or promises to give to man everything that he can dream of—and even that which is beyond his imagination—why should he remain opposed to it? The system does not cause him pain but rather pleasure. The people therefore recognize themselves in their commodities; they find their soul in their automobile, hi-fi set, split-level home, kitchen equipment. Technology creates a false man, a man who learns how to find happiness in what is given to him by the system. His soul is created as the image of what he can have. To the extent to which the system creates new needs and provides the objects to satisfy these needs, it is able to keep man an integral part of itself. . . . The success of the system in the delivery of goods now provides the basis for the ideological justification and practical self-perpetuation. Whatever delivers goods must be true. Internal happiness requires defense against everything that is a threat from outside. Consequently, welfare state and warfare state become one, living in a harmonious symbiosis. (pp. 23–24)

Marshall McLuhan, *Counterblast*. Designed by Harley Parker

When we put satellites around the planet, Darwinian Nature ended. The earth became an art form subject to the same programming as media networks and their environments. The entire evolutionary process shifted, at the moment of Sputnik, from biology to technology. Evolution became not an involuntary response of organism to new conditions but a part of the consensus of human consciousness. Such a revolution is enormously greater and more confusing to past attitudes than anything that can confront a mere culture or civilization. THE IVORY TOWER BECOMES THE CONTROL TOWER OF HUMAN NAVIGATION. (New York: Harcourt, Brace & World, 1969, p. 143)

Hope and Revolution

Jürgen Moltmann, *Religion, Revolution, and the Future*. Trans. M. Douglas Meeks

If students are discovering today that "truth is revolutionary," Christians are discovering that the truth of Jesus "makes them free" and demands to be "done," as the Fourth Gospel says. The Christian certainty of hope becomes practical in the transformation of the present. In the expectation of divine transformation we transform ourselves and the conditions around us into the likeness of the new creation. This is a possibility—the very possibility from which Christian faith lives. This possibility is realized in repentance, in conversion, in new birth to living hope and in new life which refuses to acknowledge Godless obligations. A messianic stream of renewal runs through history from the Christ of God who died in this world and was raised into the coming new world of God's righteousness. In him there are, and always were found, not only the inner repentance and liberation of the heart but also the reformations, renaissances, and revolutions of external conditions. For Christian hope the world is not an insignificant waiting room for the soul's journey to heaven, but the "arena" of the new creation of all things and the battleground of freedom. Christian hope dare not evacuate the present by dreaming about the future; nor may it compensate for an empty present by dreaming about the future. It must, rather, draw the hoped-for future already into the misery of the present and use it in practical initiatives for overcoming this misery. Through criticism and protest, on the one hand, and creative imagination and action, on the other, we can avail ourselves of freedom for the future. (New York: Charles Scribner's Sons, 1969, pp. 139–40)

Gerald O'Collins, *Man and His New Hopes*

In our day Mao Tse-tung has set out his version of the Marxist future which has freedom from "foreign and domestic oppressors" as its pre-condition. Liberation from imperialist politico-economic exploitation and from restrictive religious and family practices, together with the change from private to common ownership, will permit the task of culture and economic construction to go ahead. "Our nation," Mao declares, "will work bravely and industriously to create its own civilization and happiness, and will at the same time promote world peace and freedom." This goal which a reorganized society and a developed economy can make possible lies in the not very distant future. "We believe that revolution can change everything and that before long there will arise a new China with a big population and a great wealth of products, where life will be abundant and culture will flourish." This coming "golden age" will mean not only the national freedom and unity of the Chinese people, but also "world peace." In words which recall Isaiah, Mao announces "the age of permanent peace," "the epoch of peaceful life during which there will never be war." (New York: Herder & Herder, 1969, p. 105)

Martin E. Marty, *The Search for a Usable Future*

Dedication to the innovative principle should be more radical than alternatives. Karl Marx in his philosophy of history lets history, in effect, come to an end "inside history"; so do all Utopias. The Christian faith cannot conceive of such a moment: the pressure from the future suggests that even revolution may not bring in a full and final resolution of history. Christians want to remain sufficiently disengaged so that they can carry change further than through a revolution. (New York, Evanston, & London: Harper & Row, 1969, p. 111)

Harvey Cox, *The Feast of Fools: A Theological Essay on Festivity and Fantasy*

The question we should be asking should run like this: Given the fact that our polis, the human community, needs a company of dreamers, seers, servants, and jesters in its midst, where shall this company come from? Given the fact that biblical imagery—Jesus, Job, Jeremiah—has produced prophets and revolutionaries in the past, how can we keep telling these stories? Given the fact that in festive ritual man's fantasy life is both fed and kept in touch with the earth, how can we eat the bread and toast the hope in ways that ring true? How can we keep restating the vision of the New Age so that the poor and persecuted continue to push and the princes and potentates never feel secure? (Cambridge: Harvard University Press, 1969, p. 96)

Bibliography

Chapter One

Balthasar, Hans Urs von. *A Theology of History.* New York: Sheed & Ward, 1963.

Barrett, William. *Irrational Man.* Garden City, N.Y.: Doubleday Anchor Books, 1962.

Cullman, Oscar. *Christ and Time.* Philadelphia: Westminster Press, 1950.

Dawson, Christopher. *Dynamics of World History.* New York: Sheed & Ward, 1956.

Driver, Tom F. *The Sense of History in Greek and Shakespearean Drama.* New York & London: Columbia University Press, 1967.

Eliade, Mircea. *Cosmos and History: The Myth of Eternal Return.* New York: Harper Torchbooks, 1959.

———. *Myth and Reality.* New York: Harper Torchbooks, 1968.

Kitto, H. D. F. *Form and Meaning in Drama.* New York: University Paperbacks, 1960.

McLuhan, Marshall. *Understanding Media: The Extensions of Man.* New York: McGraw-Hill Book Co., 1965.

Marcel, Gabriel. *Homo Viator: Introduction to a Metaphysic of Hope.* New York: Harper Torchbooks, 1962.

Moltmann, Jürgen. *Theology of Hope.* New York: Harper & Row, 1967.

Ong, Walter J., S.J. *In the Human Grain.* New York: Macmillan Co., 1967.

Rahner, Karl. "The Theology of Hope." *Theology Digest,* Sesquicentennial Issue (February, 1968): 78–87.

Wildenstein, Georges. *Gauguin.* Paris: Éditions les Beaux-Arts, 1964.

Chapter Two

Shakespeare, William. *King Lear*. The Signet Classic Shakespeare, ed. Russell Fraser. New York: The New American Library, 1963.

Beckett, Samuel. *Endgame*. New York: Grove Press, 1958.

Bradley, A. C. *Shakespearean Tragedy*. London: Macmillan & Co., 1904; New York: St. Martin's Press, 1905.

Elton, William R. *King Lear and the Gods*. San Marino, Calif.: The Huntington Library, 1966.

Goddard, Harold C. *The Meaning of Shakespeare*. Vol. 2. 1st Phoenix Books ed. Chicago: University of Chicago Press, 1960.

Harrison, G. B. *Shakespeare's Tragedies*. London: Routledge & Kegan Paul, 1951; New York: Oxford University Press, 1969.

Heilman, Robert B. *This Great Stage*. Baton Rouge: Louisiana State University Press, 1948.

Knight, G. Wilson. *The Wheel of Fire*. 4th ed. London: Methuen & Co., 1949.

Kott, Jan. *Shakespeare Our Contemporary*. Garden City, N.Y.: Doubleday Anchor Books, 1966.

Lynch, William F., S.J. *Images of Hope*. New York & Toronto: Mentor-Omega Books, 1966.

McLuhan, Marshall. *The Gutenberg Galaxy*. Toronto: University of Toronto Press, 1965.

Spencer, Theodore. *Shakespeare and the Nature of Man*. 2nd ed. New York: Macmillan Co., 1949.

Welsford, Enid. *The Fool: His Social and Literary History*. London: Faber & Faber, 1935; Gloucester, Mass.: Peter Smith, 1966.

Chapter Three

Strindberg, August. *The Confession of a Fool (Le Plaidoyer d'un fou)*. Translated by Ellie Scheussner. Boston: Small, Maynard & Co., 1913.

———. *Inferno*. Translated by Mary Sandbach. Introduction by F. L. Lucas. London: Hutchinson & Co., 1962.

———. *Inferno, Alone and Other Writings*. Edited and introduced by Evert Sprinchorn. Garden City, N.Y.: Doubleday Anchor Books, 1968.

———. *To Damascus* I. Translated by Evert Sprinchorn. *The Genius of the Scandinavian Theater.* Edited and with an Introduction by Evert Sprinchorn. New York: Mentor Books, 1964.

———. *To Damascus* I, II, III. *Eight Expressionist Plays.* Translated and with Preface to the Pilgrimage Plays by Arvid Paulson. Introduction and Preface to *The Ghost Sonata* by John Gassner. New York: Bantam Books, 1965.

Dahlstrom, Carl E. W. L. "Situation and Character in *Till Damaskus.*" *PMLA* LIII (1939): 886–902.

Eliade, Mircea. *Myths, Dreams and Mysteries.* Translated by Philip Mairet. New York: Harper Torchbooks, 1967.

Fergusson, Francis. *Dante's Drama of the Mind.* Princeton, N.J.: Princeton University Press, 1968.

Frankl, Viktor E. *The Doctor and the Soul.* Translated by Richard and Clara Winston. 2nd ed., with revisions and added chapter written in English by the author. New York: Bantam Books, 1967.

Kierkegaard, S. *Repetition.* Translated with Introduction and Notes by Walter Lowrie. Princeton, N.J.: University Press, 1941.

Lamm, Martin. *August Strindberg.* Stockholm, 1928.

Singleton, Charles. *An Essay on the Vita Nuova.* Cambridge, Mass.: Harvard University Press, 1949.

Thomte, Reidar. *Kierkegaard's Philosophy of Religion.* Princeton, N.J.: Princeton University Press, 1949.

Williams, Raymond. *Drama from Ibsen to Eliot.* Middlesex, England: Penguin Books, 1964, 1967; New York: Oxford University Press, 1969. First published London: Chatto & Windus, 1952.

Chapter Four

Eliot, T. S. *The Cocktail Party.* New York: A Harvest Book, Harcourt, Brace & World, 1950.

———. *The Complete Poems and Plays, 1909–1950.* New York: Harcourt, Brace & World, 1952.

———. *The Idea of a Christian Society.* New York: Harcourt, Brace & World, 1939.

———. *Selected Essays, 1917–1932.* New York: Harcourt, Brace & Co., 1932.

Arrowsmith, William. "English Verse Drama II: *The Cocktail Party*." *The Hudson Review* III, No. 3 (Autumn, 1950): 411–30.

Bentley, Eric. *The Dramatic Event*. New York: Horizon Press, 1954.

Browne, E. Martin. *The Making of a Play*. Cambridge: University Press, 1966.

Hailey, Foster. "An Interview with T. S. Eliot." *The New York Times*, April 16, 1950, Section 2, p. 1.

Hall, Donald. "T. S. Eliot: The Art of Poetry I" (Interview). *Paris Review* XXI (Spring-Summer, 1959): 47–70.

Headings, Philip R. *T. S. Eliot*. New York: Twayne Publishers, 1964.

Heilman, Robert B. "*Alcestis* and *The Cocktail Party*," *Comparative Literature* V (Spring, 1955): 105–16.

Hirai, Masao, ed. with Tomlin, E. W. F. *T. S. Eliot: A Tribute from Japan*. Tokyo: The Kenyusha Press, 1966.

Knust, Herbert. "What's the Matter with One-Eyed Riley?" *Comparative Literature* XVII, No. 4 (Fall, 1965): 289–98.

Lynch, William F., S.J. *Christ and Apollo: The Dimensions of the Literary Imagination*. New York: Sheed & Ward, 1960; A Mentor-Omega Book, 1963.

Martz, Louis L. "The Wheel and the Point: Aspects of Imagery and Theme in Eliot's Later Poetry." *The Sewanee Review*, Winter, 1947: 126–47.

McLaughlin, John J., S.J. "A Daring Metaphysic: *The Cocktail Party*." *Renascence* III, No. 1 (Autumn, 1950): 15–28.

Otto, Rudolf. *The Idea of the Holy*. New York & London: Oxford University Press, 1958; first published in 1923.

Pound, Ezra, and Fenollosa, Ernest. *The Classic Noh Theatre of Japan*. New York: New Directions, 1959.

Robbins, Rossell Hope. *The T. S. Eliot Myth*. New York: Henry Schuman, 1951.

Smith, Grover, Jr. *T. S. Eliot's Poetry and Plays*. Chicago: University of Chicago Press, 1950 and 1956.

Smith, R. Gregor. "An Exchange of Notes on T. S. Eliot." *Theology Today* VII, No. 4 (January, 1951): 503–6.

Williams, Raymond. *Drama from Ibsen to Eliot*. Middlesex, England: Penguin Books, 1964, 1967; New York: Oxford University Press, 1969.

Wimsatt, W. K., Jr., ed. *English Stage Comedy*. New York: Columbia University Press, 1955.

Chapter Five

Claudel, Paul. *Oeuvres complètes,* vol. 11. Paris: Gallimard, 1957. Contains the "première version" (written in 1905) of *Partage de Midi,* the "version pour la scène" used by Jean-Louis Barrault in the 1948 production and the "nouvelle version pour la scène," 1949, plus a number of notes and letters.

———. *Break of Noon,* translation of the "nouvelle version pour la scène." Translated and with an Introduction by Wallace Fowlie. Chicago: Henry Regnery Co., Gateway Edition, 1960.

———. *Oeuvres complètes,* vol. 1. *Corona Benignitatis Anni Dei.* Paris: Gallimard, 1915. Contains "Ténèbres."

———. *The Correspondence 1899–1926 between Paul Claudel and André Gide.* Introduction and Notes by Robert Mallet. Prefaced and translated by John Russell. London: Secker & Warburg, 1952.

———. *Mémoires improvisés,* with J. Amrouche. Paris: Gallimard, 1954.

———. *Oeuvres complètes,* vol. 12. *Le Soulier de satin (texte pour la scène).* Paris: Gallimard, 1944.

———. *The Satin Slipper.* Translation of the original text by the Rev. John O'Connor with the collaboration of the author. New Haven: Yale University Press, 1931.

Brereton, Geoffrey. *Principles of Tragedy.* Coral Gables, Fla.: University of Miami Press, 1968.

Guicharnaud, Jacques, in collaboration with June Guicharnaud. *Modern French Theatre from Giraudoux to Genet.* New Haven & London: Yale University Press, 1967.

Madaule, Jacques. *Le Drame de Paul Claudel.* Paris: Desclée, 1936.

Marcel, Gabriel. *Regards sur le théâtre de Claudel.* Paris: Beauchesne, 1964.

Peyre, Henri. "A Dramatist of Genius." *Chicago Review* XV (Autumn, 1961): 71–78.

Chapter Six

Williams, Tennessee. *Camino Real.* Norfolk, Conn.: New Directions, 1953.

———. "The Timeless World of a Play." Published with *The Rose Tattoo.* New York: New Directions, 1951.

Eliade, Mircea. *Cosmos and History: The Myth of Eternal Return.* New York: Harper Torchbooks, 1959.

Groote, Gerard. *The Following of Christ.* (Usually associated with a later editor of the work, Thomas à Kempis.) Translated into English by Joseph Malaise, S.J., from original Netherlandish texts as edited by James van Ginneken, S.J. New York: America Press, 1937.

Jackson, Esther Merle. *The Broken World of Tennessee Williams.* Madison, Milwaukee & London: University of Wisconsin Press, 1966.

Teilhard de Chardin, Pierre. *The Divine Milieu.* New York: Harper Torchbooks, 1955.

Vowles, Richard B. "Tennessee Williams and Strindberg." *Modern Drama* I (December, 1958): 166–71.

Chapter Seven

Ionesco, Eugène. *Théâtre,* vol. 4. *Le Roi se meurt, La Soif et la faim,* etc. Paris: Gallimard, 1966.

———. *Hunger and Thirst and Other Plays.* Translated by Donald Watson. New York: Grove Press, 1969.

———. *Notes and Counter Notes: Writings on the Theatre.* Translated by Donald Watson. New York: Grove Press, 1964.

Boisdeffre, Pierre de. "Plaidoyer pour Ionesco," a reply to Gabriel Marcel's review. *Les Nouvelles littéraires,* April 7, 1966, p. 13.

Bonnefoy, Claude. *Entretiens avec Eugène Ionesco.* Paris: Éditions Pierre Belfond, 1966.

C.C. "Ionesco et Les Subventions." *Les Nouvelles littéraires,* February 24, 1966, p. 13.

Eliade, Mircea. *Myths, Dreams, and Mysteries.* Translated by Philip Mairet. New York: Harper Torchbooks, 1967.

Genêt (Janet Flanner). "Letter from Paris." *The New Yorker,* July 16, 1966, pp. 101–102.

Guicharnaud, Jacques, in collaboration with June Guicharnaud. *Modern French Theatre from Giraudoux to Genet.* New Haven & London: Yale University Press, 1967.

Jacobsen, Josephine, and Mueller, William R. *Ionesco and Genet.* New York: Hill & Wang, 1968.

Marcel, Gabriel. *Homo Viator: Introduction to a Metaphysic of Hope.* Translated by Emma Craufurd. New York: Harper Torchbooks, 1962.

———. "Une Mesure pour rien," review of *La Soif et la faim. Les Nouvelles littéraires,* March 10, 1966, p. 13.

Triolet, Elsa. "A Chromo by Ionesco." *Atlas* XI (May, 1966): 311–13. Translated from *Les Lettres Françaises,* Paris.

Chapter Eight

Betti, Ugo. "Essays, Correspondence, Notes." Translated by William Meriwether and Gino Rizzo. *TDR, The Drama Review* VIII, No. 3 (Spring, 1964): 51–86.

———. *Raccolta di novelle.* Bologna: Cappelli, 1963.

———. *Religione e Teatro.* With a dedication by Andreina Betti. Brescia: Morcelliana, 1957.

———. "Religion and the Theater." Translated by Gino Rizzo and William Meriwether. *TDR* V, No. 2 (December, 1960): 3–14. Reprinted in *Masterpieces of the Modern Italian Theatre.* Ed. Robert W. Corrigan. New York: Collier Books, 1967, pp. 171–81.

———. *Teatro completo.* Prefaces by Silvio D'Amico and Achille Fiocco. Bologna: Cappelli, 1957.

———. *Three Plays on Justice (Landslide, Struggle Till Dawn, The Fugitive).* Translated, with an introductory essay, by G. H. McWilliam. San Francisco: Chandler Publishing Co., 1964.

Buber, Martin. *Eclipse of God.* New York: Harper & Brothers, 1952.

Cologni, Franco. *Documenti di teatro: Ugo Betti.* Bologna: Cappelli, 1960.

Fergusson, Francis. *Dante's Drama of the Mind.* Princeton, N.J.: Princeton University Press, 1968.

Lynch, William F., S.J. *Images of Hope.* New York & Toronto: Mentor-Omega Books, 1966.

Marcel, Gabriel. *Homo Viator: Introduction to a Metaphysic of Hope.* Translated by Emma Craufurd. New York: Harper Torchbooks, 1962.

Chapter Nine

Lowell, Robert. *The Old Glory*. Introduction by Robert Brustein. Director's Note by Jonathan Miller. New York: The Noonday Press, a division of Farrar, Straus and Giroux, 1965.

———. *For the Union Dead*. New York: Farrar, Straus and Giroux, 1965.

Alvarez, A. "A Talk with Robert Lowell." *Encounter* XXIV (February, 1965): 39–43.

Clebsch, William A. *From Sacred to Profane America*. New York: Harper & Row, 1968.

The Jerusalem Bible. Ed. Alexander Jones. Garden City, N.Y.: Doubleday & Co., 1966.

Kott, Jan. *Shakespeare Our Contemporary*. Garden City, N.Y.: Doubleday Anchor Books, 1966.

Hawthorne, Nathaniel. *Great Short Works of Nathaniel Hawthorne*. A Perennial Classic. Edited, with an Introduction, by Frederick C. Crews. New York: Harper & Row, 1967.

Hochman, Baruch. "Robert Lowell's *The Old Glory*." *TDR* XI (Summer, 1967): 127–38.

Miller, Perry. *Errand into the Wilderness*. Cambridge, Mass.: The Belknap Press of Harvard University Press, 1956.

Pearce, Roy Harvey. "Hawthorne and the Sense of the Past, or, the Immortality of Major Molineux." *Journal of English Literary History* XXI (December, 1954): 327–49.

Smith, Cleveland H., and Taylor, Gertrude R. *Flags of All Nations*. New York: Thomas Y. Crowell Co., 1946.